Daily Spiritual Pray

Written By
Rachelle Sat'chell

Guided By The Holy Spirit In Me

Nothing is unreachable except
the things that we don't reach for.
Reach for the God who is
always available, always on time,
and always willing to supply
our every need.

xulon
PRESS

Copyright © 2006 by Rachelle Sat'chell

Daily I Will Pray
by Rachelle Sat'chell

Printed in the United States of America

ISBN 1-59781-818-6

Library of Congress Number Txu1-226-930

ALL RIGHTS RESERVED under International
Copyright Law. The author guarantees all contents are
original and do not infringe upon the legal rights of
any other person or work. No portion of this book
may be reproduced in any form, or transmitted in
any form without written permission from the Author,
except as provided by United States of America
copyright law. The views expressed in this book
are not necessarily those of the publisher.

Unless otherwise indicated, all Scripture quotations are
taken from the King James Version of the HTML Bible.

Rachelle Sat'chell Ministries
Central Park Post Office
P.O. Box 1233
Buffalo, New York 14215-1233

E-mail address: Virtuous1972@yahoo.com

www.xulonpress.com

Presented To:

_____

With the Love of Christ

From:

_____

Date:

_____

To God be the Glory

Acknowledgments

WITH SPECIAL THANKS:

♥ PRAISE AND THANKS TO MY HEAVENLY FATHER

♥ Pastor Bronner, my Pastor, Spiritual director, Father, Teacher

♥ To my best friend, Kevin, for your continued support in all that is important to me. Thank you for visualizing me from the inside out. Thank you for your continued patience, loyalty, kindness, dedication, and unconditional love that has kept me, and keeps me expanding my knowledge of God's potential for me. I appreciate you and love you.

♥ To my sisters: Nakisha, Bridgette and Rhonda. Thank you for individually being the best that you can be for me and for others. Thank you for loving me in spite of myself. Thank you for supporting me, and for not only being my sisters, but my friends.

♥ To all of my prayer partners too numerous to name, thank you. Thank you for your e-mails of testimonies describing how my writing has helped you. Thank you for continuing to encourage me in my writing. It is those e-mails that encouraged me to continue to write and create this book.

♥ To all of my friends, Pastor Raymond &Vanessa Dixson, Tom Gardner, Robert Hayes, Robert Weinrib, Rick Quinn, Anthony Fitzgerald and most of all my Mom. Without all of you, this book would have been much harder to pull together. Thank you for making it easier for me. Thank you for allowing the spirit to move within you on my behalf. Thank you for your reading, editing, resources and your continued assistance.

♥ Thank you Pastor Raymond, Vanessa and Tom for pushing me past my comfort zone and into God's zone for my life.

♥ Thank you Robert (Bobbo) for your patience through the numerous changes to get the best results.

♥ Thank you MARK PEARCE for your artistic inspiration. I did what I love, I acted on what I love and here is the result. Your TURN!!!

I APPRECIATE ALL OF YOU NOT ONLY FOR WHAT YOU HAVE DONE FOR ME, BUT ALSO FOR WHOM YOU ARE TO ME! TO GOD BE THE GLORY!

Giving Honor

❤ I would like to first give honor where honor is due. Honor is first due to my omni-present Father, the lover of my soul, my first husband, my way maker, my heart fixer, my mind regulator, my bridge over troubled waters my, my, my, what honor is due. I honor Him, my Lord and Savior, my ever-present help. God has been all that I need and has promised to never leave me or forsake me. I honor Him for helping me die to my fleshly desires that I might live through Him, that I might live life exceedingly abundantly above the life that I have set for myself. I would like to give honor to my Pastor, T. Anthony Bronner. A man who has been one of my pathways to learning how to reach my heavenly Father. He has assisted me in my development and my ability to continue to grow and mature in God. I HONOR HIM!

❤ I would like to honor my children, **WHOM I DEDI-CATE THIS BOOK TO. My Daughter,** a young woman who watched me go from one addiction to the next. I honor her because although for most of her life, this was her example, she never chose to follow in my footsteps. As a teenager, I see that she is choosing to follow in the footsteps of her new mother who's addicted to Christ. **(2Corinthians 5:17) "Therefore if any man be in Christ, he is a new creature: old things are passed away; behold, all things have become new."** I HONOR HER! My **Son,** a young man who was born two months before his scheduled due date. He spent the first few years of his life sick. The doctors said he'd have problems until his inner body caught up with his outer body. He was a big healthy looking child, but he struggled with his breathing, hearing and speaking. I honor him because against all the odds in his life, his strength over came it all. The strength given to Him by God, and at a very early age he recognized his source. He verbalizes that through powerful prayer that ignites anyone within earshot of hearing him. I HONOR HIM.

♥ I would like to honor my **Mother, Maureen**. My mother is a woman who exemplifies strength and unconditional love. I HONOR HER. I honor **Jim** for being great in all that you do for me and for my Mom.

♥ I would like to honor my **Father, Edward**. My Father, who in his own way, taught me a great deal about the characteristics of being a good woman. I HONOR HIM!

♥ Lastly, but not at all least, I'd like to honor another spiritual Father and his wife my spiritual sister (**Pastor Raymond&Vanessa Dixson**). I honor them for leading me to Christ and guiding me to this place of maturity. I honor Vanessa for FEELING me regardless of where I was or where I am. God has given her the ability to FEEL me from near or far. I HONOR THEM! To God be the GLORY!

Preface

∼

I will bless the Lord at all times and His praises shall
continually be in my mouth. I serve an awesome
God who is truly worthy of all my praise. I pray that no flesh
shall Glory from these words shared. I am writing these
prayers as a vessel of my Lord and Savior Jesus Christ. It is
my life; the process, trials, tribulations, valleys and mountains that God has brought me through that have developed
these prayers. My life has been written in these words.

Every day for the last four years, I wrote prayers that
would guide me, lead me and encourage me to keep going,
to continue on the path of greatness that GOD has predestined me to walk on. I share this process with you that God
might use these prayers to do the same for every eye that
views these pages.

I come through these words to meet you where you are,
no matter if it is in the desert, a land where you are desperate for water. If it is in the wilderness where you have hid-
den yourself that you might be removed from the pains and
pressures of the world. No matter if it is on top of the mountain where you are standing because you have worked hard
to get there and you recognize your need to be close to God.
If it is in the street where you have chosen to stay because it
is all you know. No matter what street you are on, I guaran-
tee you that there is something in this book that will make
you feel like I'm all in your business, where your heart flut-

ters because you realize that someone understands and has had the same experience that you are experiencing right now. Not one of these prayers was written with the intention to help anyone other than me, but God has spoke a word to me that He will use them to also help YOU.

So, I give to you on this day, words that you can read with your eyes, hear in your spirit and feel in your heart that God will be glorified. God has given me a word in my heart, that I have written in this book, that you might read and be encouraged, equipped, energized, excited, eager, enthusiastic and expecting change in you and around you. In these words written in this book, is your equipment to grow, prosper and have peace and joy as you go through the purging, processes, and possibilities of life. **(Is. 40:29) "God gives power to the weak, and to those who have no might he increases strength."**

I Surrender

*I*t is my honor to have you reading this book. I am a woman who has decided to be a living sacrifice. I have surrendered my will and all of my ways to my God, the lover of my soul, the God who has made me whole. It took me many years to realize how much I needed Him to be Lord over every area of my life. Since that day I have been focused on serving Him. I have been through the valley, over the mountain, and in the wilderness.

When I was of the world I used different addictions to survive-life. Now that I have surrendered my life to Christ no matter how deep the valley is, how high the mountain is, or how long the wilderness, at last I have peace. I have peace as I allow the Holy Spirit to guide me every step of the way.

As God leads me through the day and holds me through the night, I submit and SURRENDER to Him. I am driven by His unconditional love. I am encouraged by His gentle push that has kept me moving forward in the way in which He has for me to go. I have been pruned, pressed, positioned, poked, primed, processed, and on the potter's wheel that He might use me to speak to you.

I have a testimony of His grace, love and mercy, and it is because of that testimony that my heart speaks in every word that is written. I am an example that the potter can change nothing into something. He has put the shattered pieces of my heart back together and He has loved me in spite of myself.

I am humbled and grateful that He is using me to meet you where you are that you might get to where He has predestined you to go **(Is. 40:29) "God gives power to the weak, and to those who have no might he increases strength."** (Is. 61: 1-2) **"The Spirit of the Sovereign Lord is on me, because the Lord has anointed me to preach good news to the poor. He sent me to bind up the BROKENHEARTED, to proclaim FREEDOM for the captives and release from darkness the prisoners, to proclaim the YEAR of the Lord's FAVOR."**

Introduction

I welcome you to my first book **"Daily I Will Pray "** No matter where you are or what you are going through God is just a prayer a way. There is a God who sits on the throne and awaits our invitation, an invitation that welcomes Him into our lives. God is not a God who judges us on our past and/or present. He is a God who loves us in spite of our self. Welcoming Him in is the first step to letting Him know we desire to be better and to do better in our life.

God has been with us many times before we even knew He was there. It is God who saved us from things we overlooked, but now we look back and ask ourselves "How did I get through that?" It was God. He created us and loves us in spite of our mistakes. It is essential before you pray that you invite Jesus into every area of your life. If you have invited Him in and He already lives inside of you then be patient that other sisters and brothers learn how to welcome Him into their lives.

Lord Jesus, I need You. I thank You for dying on the cross for my sins. I open the door of my life and my heart to You. I receive You as my Lord, my Savior, and my King. I repent for my sins and ask that You forgive me. I give You complete control of my life and I surrender my will for Yours. I give You the authority to change my life and give me all that I need to endure the change. I thank You for loving me and I ask that You dwell with in me and, refresh, restore, renew and rejuvenate me. Amen! **For those of you who have just prayed this prayer I ask that you e-mail me @ virtuous1972@yahoo.com and share the experience with me and receive some additional information. Please put "Inviting Jesus" in the subject heading.**

Now that we are all on the same page and we all have a personal relationship with Jesus, it is imperative that we keep it personal. When we pray God wants us to talk with Him. He wants us to talk to Him as a Father and/or a friend. He wants us to be honest with Him because He already knows what's in our heart, so speak freely. A part of praying is sharing with God how you are feeling and then requesting that He help you where you are. He waits for us. God is not a God who will invade our lives and take charge. He is gentle, compassionate and He waits to be invited.

So, when you need Him, call Him. He is the only one who will never be too busy to take your call. Be honest, be open and be ready for Him to change your life. If He doesn't respond right away, be patient and draw your strength from Him. We can pray about anything and God loves when we pray about everything. He is always near and we've invited Him into our life. Allow Him in every area and don't seclude Him to only your problems. We can pray and thank Him, tell Him how much we love Him and share our joys with Him. He wants to provide everything we need and He wants us to desire to spend time with Him daily in prayer. Start today! SHALL WE...

Why God?

〜

*T*here are things that God requires us to go through that we might be built from the inside out, that we might understand all of the promises of who He is to us. A part of believing in His promises is knowing who He is and experiencing Him for ourselves. So, when the word says that: **(Ps.147:3) "He healeth the broken heart, and bindeth up their wounds."** If we have never been broken hearted then how would we know that He is a healer?

When the word says that: **(Is.53:4) " Surely He hath borne our griefs, and carried our sorrows."** How do we know that He will carry our sorrows if we've never had sorrows given to Him to carry?

When the word says: **(John 14:27) "Peace I leave with you, my peace I give unto you: not as the world giveth, give I unto you. Let not your heart be troubled, neither let it be afraid."** How do we know that God will give us peace when we are afraid or troubled if we've never had any fear or trouble?

When the word says: **(Is. 40:29) "He giveth power to the faint; and to them that have no might he increaseth strength."** How do we know that God will strengthen us when we are feeling weak if we have never had weak moments? When the word says: **(Jer.30:17) "For I will restore health unto thee, and I will heal thee of thy wounds, saith the Lord;"** How do we know God as a healer if we have never been sick and/or wounded?

When the word says: **(Jer.31:13b)" I will turn their mourning into joy, and will comfort them, and make them rejoice from their sorrow..."** How do we know God as a comforter and an author of our joy if we have never had any mourning or sorrow?

God wants us to know Him intimately. He wants us to allow Him to be all that we need and everything that we want. Intimately He wants us to be secure, satisfied, settled and simplified in His arms the arms that He wraps around us as He turns our process into possibilities our hurt into healing, our sorrows into successes, our pain into power, our sickness into strength, our wounds into words.

I have been through it all and through it all God has given me a word in due season to open the doors of your heart that He might be your hearts desire. That you will grow intimately knowing that He is the best lover for your soul. That He might be all that He has promised to be and all that He will prove to be if you let Him. He is faithful! GLORY! GLORY! to His wonderful, awesome and powerful name.

No Name

*G*lory to the most high, my heart is on fire and it won't
go out, my desire is for more of Him. I have a passion for more and more of Jesus in my life. I want Him in
every room in my house. I need Him to guide me, see for
me, hear for me and teach me to love for Him.

I love the Lord with all my soul. I thank Him for seeing
me for who I have become and changing me into who He
wants me to be. I praise Him and worship Him because I
recognize Him and His good works in my life. **(Ps.149:1)**
**"Praise ye the Lord. Sing unto the Lord a new song, and
praise in the congregation of saints."**

I went to a church service one night and it was an awesome experience. During the service, I heard my Pastor
(T.Anthony Bronner) preaching out of Luke. He spoke about
the disciples who knew that Jesus rose from the dead, yet
they still decided to leave to go to a land that geographically
didn't even exist because it was some NO NAMED
WOMAN who told them that He had risen. As I absorbed
the word I captured a different message for myself. I used to
see myself as a NO NAMED WOMAN and that's still the
way, looking at my history, people see me. I'm not a woman
who has a big family name, who grew up in a sanctified
church, who grew up rich-in anything, who grew up in a loving and functional family, who has known Jesus all of my
life. No I'm not that woman. I'm the woman with a past, the

woman who recognized Jesus in my life at 26.

I spent most of my life as a NO NAMED WOMAN. BUT GOD, is using me through the pain of my past. Don't miss the word because I have NO NAME. There is no preacher or bishop before my name, but there is a name written all over my heart, in which I speak to you from. That name is JESUS.

I pray that you don't miss the word when it's for you even when it's coming from a person with no name, that you look through the mirror that God is looking at you through, and know that regardless of what people think, God has plans to use you. That you see a person in that mirror that is beautifully and wonderfully made and He wants to use you to show people His marvelous works.

I pray that you too will let God use your past for someone else's future, that you too will be healed of your past and allow God to work some good from it in the lives of the people around you. **(Is. 61: 1-2) "The Spirit of the Lord GOD is upon me; because the LORD hath anointed me to preach good tidings unto the meek; he hath sent me to bind up the brokenhearted, to proclaim liberty to the captives, and the opening of the prison to them that are bound; To proclaim the acceptable year of the LORD, and the day of vengeance of our God; to comfort all that mourn"**

Although the sermon was more about being out of God's will because of our disappointment, the disciples were disappointed that the man (Jesus) they SAW do miracles, died. The man who they looked at as powerful, died. So they put distance between themselves and God. How we to can put distance between God and ourselves because of our disappointment. How our disappointment can take us right out of the will of God because our focus is no longer God, but it is our disappointment.

Although I grasped the word, I grasped another word as well. I was consumed with the piece that they didn't listen to the NO NAMED WOMAN. To GOD be the GLORY!!!

Additional no name woman: Jeremiah 4:31, 6:24, 13:21, 22:23, 30:6, Hosea13:13, Micah 4:9-10 – no named women who knew how to travail (cry-out). Matthew 9:20-22, Mark 5:25-33 – no named women who had some issues that pressed forward to find the healer. Matthew 15:22-28 – a no named woman whose faith got her daughter healed Matthew 27: 6:10- a woman who served the Lord with her tears.

Reflections:

Trusting in Him

∼

We serve a faithful God. He is awesome and worthy to be praised. Magnify Him with me. Give Him Glory. Give Him honor for He is worthy. Praise Him. Let the meditation of our heart be pleasing to Him. Glory. Jesus is wonderful.

Thank you Jesus for the blood. Thank you for your grace and mercy that is new to us every morning. Thank you Lord for being all that I have needed you to be when I needed you to be it.

Praise Your Holy and wonderful name. There is no one like You. You are wonderful and magnificent. **(Isaiah 25:1) "O Lord, Thou art God; I will exalt Thee, I will praise Thy name; for Thou hast done wonderful things;"**

I come to you filled with the joy of the LORD because He is so awesome and worthy of all my praises. I thank God that I'm not where I used to be. I thank God that in Him I can put my complete trust. I pray that on this day we would TRUST HIM, that we would trust Him for the big things and trust Him for the small things, that in all we say and do we would trust Him because He knows us better than we know ourselves and we can trust Him. **(1Peter 5:7) "Casting all your care upon him; for he careth for you."** Casting means to roll over. I pray: that we all roll over any broken-ness, unforgiveness, fear, doubt, worry, disappointments and hurt to Him, that from this day forth we all would roll over everything, not hold anything back that we can't handle alone anyway. He has a plan for our lives we just have to seek Him in EVERYTHING, for all things, allow Him to: clear our mind, direct our steps and purge our spirit. I encourage you not to allow anything from your past experiences impact your future blessings. To God be the Glory!

Additional References: Job39:11, 2Samuel22:3, Ps.5:11, 2Corinthians1:9

Reflections:

Walk in His Light

❦

Praise Him for He is worthy! He kept me so I wouldn't give up. His grace and mercy kept me. Isn't God awesome! Isn't He worthy of all our praises! Isn't He worthy to be thanked and glorified! Oh come on agree with me right now, right in this moment!

I am thankful that His mercy is new every morning. I sit as a hungry servant at His feet seeking to be obedient to His will. I give Him all the Glory and Honor. No flesh shall be glorified in anything I say or do.

He is the master of my words, the keeper of my mind, the love in my heart, and the confidence in my walk, the smile on my face and whom I chase.

Prepare your hearts and minds for a word from the keeper of your mind, lover of your soul, and the God who offers wholeness. **(Hebrews 13:15) "By Him therefore let us offer the sacrifice of praise to God continually, that is, the fruit of our lips giving thanks to His name."**

It is time to say what you mean and mean what you say. It is time to walk the walk of salvation. It is time to do in spite of. We are the head and not the tail, above and not beneath, strong and not weak, the light of Jesus in the midst of darkness.

I pray that God would heal the hurting, give direction and peace to the confused. When we walk in the light of the Lord, blessings abound for us in each moment. Sometimes though we have to deliberately look for them. God's light does not blind us, but we can be blind to God's light. We don't always see the whole truth. Sometimes we see everything but the truth.

I pray that the blinders of this world be taken off of us. I pray that we get tunnel vision today. That all we see is the light of the Lord and through that light He shows us His will for our life and we walk in it. As we walk in His will He will bless us above and beyond all that we could ever think or ask for.

I pray that we would continue to walk in His strength, peace and comfort. God wants to bless us with His presence that WE MIGHT BE FILLED WITH Him internally and that we would allow Him to come out of us externally. He is strong and mighty and through Him we must be too. To God be the Glory!

Additional References: Ps.89:15, Ps.112:4, Isaiah 60:1, Micah 7:8

Reflections:

Fear

I choose to bless the Lord. I choose to allow Him to have complete control over me. I cast my care over to Him because I know that it is in Him that I can completely surrender to. I thank Him for loving me in spite of myself. I thank Him that in all things God is still God in my life. I praise Him for He is wonderful. **(Ps. 9:1) " I will praise thee, O Lord, with my whole heart; I will shew forth all thy marvelous works."**

Fear is False Evidence Appearing Real. Fear is the opposite of Faith. I pray that we will not let our fear make us miss our blessing. When we stop fearing it is because we are confident in our God. It is God who can free us from staying stagnant in our fear. I pray that we will not allow our minds to battle in fear. Get FREE: Free from the when and how. If God said it we can do it. **(Ps.51:12) "Restore unto me the joy of thy salvation; and uphold me with thy free spirit."** The Bible says that we will do greater things than Jesus did. We can't do anything Great Afraid.

I pray that we will give God total control. It is when He is in control that we no longer have to fear anything because He will direct our steps and guide our ways. Give up control and refuse to fear.

I pray that we would give the control to our Father, our heavenly Father who wants the very best for us. If we stay in control then we are at risk of missing our blessings.

Sometimes when our control is shaken we begin to fear, but when God is in control all we have to do is have faith and believe that with God all things are possible. I pray that we would allow God to be Lord over every area of our lives, committing everything to Him and allowing Him to show us any area where we are not being obedient to His will. I pray: that we would not be afraid to give God control and I know that God will direct our path if we submit to Him, that we would pray daily and ask God for direction so that we don't have to fear anything, that we would daily surrender control to our Father because we can't go wrong with Him in control. To get is to acquire or take...When we get something we obtain it by struggle or effort. When we receive something, we obtain it by acting as a receptacle and taking in what someone else is offering. Receive what Jesus pours out: Love, Mercy, Guidance, Direction, Peace, Knowledge and Grace. He did not give us a Spirit of fear, but He gave us a sound mind and a will to choose Him and His will for our lives. To God be the Glory!

Additional References: Isaiah 58:6, Colossians 3:11, Joel 2:21, Mark 4:39-40, "Out Of Control and Loving It" by Lisa Bevere, Straight Talk on Fear by Joyce Meyer

Reflections:

Identify the Enemy

*G*od is Good all the time. I praise Him for all that He has done for me. I thank Him for His grace and mercy. I worship Him for who He is in my life.

He is a restorer, a way maker, a heart fixer and a mind regulator. He is faithful and He is just. His plan is perfect. He is my Savior and my redeemer. **(Ps.107:1) "O Give thanks unto the Lord, for he is good: for his mercy endureth for ever."**

Recognize the Enemy. Identify Him and know what He is... He is a liar. The devil comes to KILL, STEAL and DESTROY. God comes that we may have life and have it MORE ABUNDANTLY. Let the devil know that you recognize that it is him who makes you worry, scared, double-minded, insecure, haughty and filled with the wrong attitude. Recognize him and know that he gives you the opposite to what God wants you to have and the longer you sit on the stair of hell welcoming these characteristics, the longer you are out of God's will for your life, the longer you will sit blinded by who you have given control to.

I pray that right in this moment we get a clear understanding of the devil and we get a clear understanding of God that we would break free from the chains of the devil and we would walk in VICTORY. **(Ps. 71:1) "In thee, O Lord, do I put my trust; let me never be put to confusion."**

VICTORY is ours but God is not going to make us take

it. We have to choose to. **(2Timothy 2: 26) "And that they may recover themselves out of the snare of the devil, who are taken captive by him at his will. " (1Peter 5: 9) "Whom resist steadfast in the faith, knowing that the same afflictions are accomplished in your brethren that are in the world." (Proverbs 10: 25) "As the whirlwind passeth, so is the wicked no more: but the righteous is an everlasting foundation." (Ps. 18: 17) "He delivered me from my strong enemy."**

Serve notice on the devil and let him know that "you are not the one." He should have killed us while he had the chance, but now that we have the word down inside of us, we are going to use it as our sword to fight. Use it to defeat Him! We are more than conquerors through Christ Jesus. We are victorious! We have the light of our Lord and Savior shining through us. To God be the Glory!

Additional References: 2Corinthians 2:11, Acts 26:18, The Word, The Blood, The Power by Joyce Meyer

Reflections:

Break the Chains...

$\mathcal{W}$e serve an awesome God. I thank Him for the breath of life. I thank Him that not only am I able to breathe but I feel refreshed knowing that I exhaled yesterday and take a breath of new grace and mercy today.

Praise God. He is great and wonderful in all that He does. His plan is perfect and His ways are excellent.

I'm thankful that everything I need I can seek Him for and get my needs met or learn patience through waiting on Him. He is whom I trust to supply all my needs in HIS TIME. **(Ps.103:1-2) "Bless the Lord, O my soul: and all that is within me, bless his holy name. Bless the Lord, O my soul, and forget not all his benefits."**

WHAT FROM YOUR PAST HAS YOU CHAINED? What is keeping you in bondage? What is not allowing you to move in the way in which you should go according to the promises of God? What painful memory won't allow your spirit to move any further? The blood has removed the chains, but the memory keeps us in bondage. Are you still walking around bound but free? You are saved from hell, but still bound by the hell of your past.

I pray: for healing right now, right in this moment, that every person reading this will recognize what their chains are and cast them over to GOD, that once we cast them over we touch them no more, that we be healed from the bruises the chains left, that the pain from our past will no longer afflict us, that God will spill His anointing into every area of our lives and leave not one area untouched by the presence of HIM, that God would give us a fresh outpouring of His spirit, that we might walk according to His direction in spite of our pain, that as we go He will heal us in a way that will strengthen us and give us the endurance to continue on the path, that we would go in the way in which He has predestined us to go in with no hindrances from the pains of this world. To God be the Glory!

Additional References: Romans12:2, 2Corinthians 11:15, 1Corinthians 1:14, 1John 1:9, He loves me He loves me not By Paula White

Reflections:

Let Us All Pray

*P*repare your hearts for prayer, clear your minds for purity, and rest in this moment knowing that the next one will be a moment of expectancy for greatness to evolve.

Father God, we come to You calling You worthy. We come with humble spirits believing that if it had not been for You we would be dead in our sin. We come to You agreeing that You are worthy and able, asking You to be good to us today even though we don't deserve it. We come to You in the mighty name of Jesus asking You to restore what the locusts and the cankerworm have destroyed.

We come trusting You and believing that You can put back together the shattered pieces of our hearts, change our vision of empty tomorrows to bright promises, and show Yourself strong by redeeming every situation that has caused us pain.

Father, we need You to break up the fowler ground and plant new seed. We fully understand that there is no one greater than You, we fill our mouths with praises unto You now, and we ask that You fill our world with Your restoration. Show Yourself strong in our lives, be Lord, be King, be our ever-present help.

Let our life be a testimony of Your grace, and we will give You the glory, praise, and honor. We will declare Your good works to everyone around us. We exalt Your name on this day calling You WORTHY FATHER, WORTHY LOVER AND WORTHY LORD! To God be the Glory!

Reflections:

Everything We Need Is In His Presence.

At all times I will GLORIFY the Lord because it is Him who is worthy to be praised for my accomplishments in life. I am a vessel who has chosen to be used by God to speak the depth of His word, to testify to the truth of His word. He is a worthy God and I am nothing without Him.

When I am lonely He wraps His arms around me and offers comfort. When I am confused, He gives me His truth, and when I am wordless, He gives me words. I thank God for His presence. I thank Him for the rest that I find in His presence. I thank Him for the fullness of joy on this day. **(Ps.118:17-21) "Shall not die, but live, and declare the works of the LORD. The LORD hath chastened me sore: but he hath not given me over unto death. Open to me the gates of righteousness: I will go into them, and I will praise the LORD: This gate of the LORD, into which the righteous shall enter. I will praise thee: for thou hast heard me, and art become my salvation."**

I pray: that we would surrender all to Him, freely give our will, trust Him, sit humbly at His feet as hungry servants, let the Holy Spirit fill us so that we may walk in divine power. Embrace the wilderness, walk within His revealed light.

I pray that we sit in His presence and let the peace that

passes all understanding fill us up until our cup overflows. **(1Chronicles 16:27) "Glory and honour are in his presence; strength and gladness are in his place."**

Whatever we are going through, God is bigger and greater than our circumstance. We can ask God to reveal to us what He wants us to learn from every situation. Climb up the mountain don't ask God to move it because then it will be behind you and that is where you have no Armor. Climb up this mountain so that it will be under your feet.

He puts us in the position that we are in so He can get the Glory when we come out. It is in the waiting, trusting and listening to Him that will bring us out. God never gives us more than we can handle, and He won't bring us out until we get what He's trying to show us.

So, draw near to Him, put your ear close to His heart and as you go through make sure you bring Him with you. We can do nothing in our own strength but we can do all things with Christ. The Joy of the Lord strengthens us to handle any and everything. God has a plan and a purpose and both work together for our good. To God be the Glory!

Additional References: 2Kings 13:23, 1 Corinthians 1:29, Hebrews11:6, Ps.37:4, Exodus 33:14, Revelation 3:20

Reflections:

His Grace

～～

We serve an awesome God. In all circumstances; trials, joys, victories, and disappointments I will lift up the name of the most high. The God of: peace, love and understanding. I thank God for His grace and mercy that bought me through. I thank Him that although I had no light to see He gave me vision. I thank Him for His strength. I thank Him that in the midst of every and anything He has given me confidence that He will NEVER leave me or forsake me for that I am forever grateful. **(Hebrews 4: 15-16) "For we have not an high priest which cannot be touched with the feeling of our infirmities; but was in all points tempted like as we are, yet without sin. Let us therefore come boldly unto the throne of grace, that we may obtain mercy, and find grace to help in time of need."**

I pray: that God would strengthen all of us in our time of weakness, that God would give us grace that is sufficient for every situation we face, that we would confidently believe that we have been called by name to do the will of the Lord and that we would stand today if not yet in Gods will, willing to be, that we would have a keen listening ear and submissive heart to walk in God's will and purpose for our lives, that we would express our love and thanksgiving towards our God who we believe in and who we believe that whatever we ask in line with His will, we shall receive in God's perfect timing in Jesus' name Amen. **(Acts 14:3) "Long** time therefore abode they speaking boldly in the Lord, which gave testimony unto the word of his grace, and granted signs and wonders to be done by their hands." (Acts 20:32) "And now, brethren, I commend you to God, and to the word of his grace, which is able to build you up, and to give you an inheritance among all them which are sanctified." (1Corinthians 15:10) "But by the grace of God I am what I am: and his grace which was bestowed upon me was not in vain; but I laboured more abundantly than they all: yet not I, but the grace of God which was with me." To God be the Glory!!!

Additional References: Romans 3:24, Galatians 1:15, Ephesians 1:6-7, Isaiah 9:6

Reflections:

Transition is Great

*G*od is worthy of my praise. He is worthy of the honor. I keep Him high and lifted up that my spirit may be the same, that I may shed some light on others that they might see His works in me. Praise God. Ooh! How wonderful is He!

I am thankful that He has supplied me the knowledge and understanding of Him. I seek more and more of Him because it is in Him that I have been set free, where I have become liberated to be and feel worthy of not only Him but worthy to do all things through Him. I'm thankful for His presence in every area of my life. He is worthy to be served with joyful obedience. I'm thankful for all assignments. I'm thankful that God has deemed me worthy to do His work. **(Ps. 103: 1-2) "Bless the LORD, O my soul: and all that is within me, bless his holy name. Bless the LORD, O my soul, and forget not all his benefits:"**

Life is a big transition; things in our lives are constantly changing. Life for Christians is nothing more than a long process, which we go through, trying to be closer and more like God. We are constantly in a process of change and newness. Transition is great. Transition is unavoidable. Transition redefines us. Transition takes time to assimilate. If Transition stops then so does growth. So, we must welcome transition. We can't allow confusion/chaos to make us lose our focus. **(Ps. 71:1) "In thee, O LORD, do I put my trust: let me never be put to confusion."**

I pray that in the midst of all transition we stay focused on God. God never changes. He is the same yesterday, today and forever. He changes the things around us to draw us closer to Him, to remind us that He is the only thing that never changes.

I pray that our daily focus be to RE PRE SENT GOD. The only way that we can do this is to stay close to Him, to know Him in all of His ways. All things work together for the good for those who love the Lord.

I pray: that we would have tunnel vision, that our entire focus be God, that we would draw near to Him that He might draw near to us, that we would walk in His will in all that we say and do, that we would have hope like Tamar, a Heart like David, Faith like Rahab, Love like Ruth, Confidence like Paul, Unlimited Grace like Bathsheba and Obedience like Mary. To God be the Glory!

Additional References: 1Corinthians 14:33, Malachi3:6, Ps.43:2-4, Romans 12:2, 2Corinthians 11:13-14, Enjoying where you are on the way to where you are going by Joyce Meyer

Reflections:

Embracing Our Lord

⊗

*T*will bless the Lord at all times and His praises shall continually be in my mouth. I thank God that I have a relationship with Him that is so intense that the challenges of this world do not intimidate me.

I refuse to allow anything to overwhelm me. I am rooted and grounded in my Lord and Savior. It is His greatness that causes me to draw to Him in the time of trouble. He is great and greatly I will praise Him for His goodness. **(Ps. 96: 1-4) " O sing unto the LORD a new song: sing unto the LORD, all the earth. Sing unto the LORD, bless his name; shew forth is salvation from day to day. Declare his glory among the heathen, his wonders among all people. For the LORD is great, and greatly to be praised."**

I pray: that we would resist the temptation to be traumatized by life, that we would choose to walk in the full assurance that the presence of God is there beside us, that we know God as an ULTIMATE Father. We have seen Him open doors for us. We have seen Him provide our every need. His word has counseled us about the things of tomorrow, and because of Him we have been made whole. I pray: that we would refuse to be stuck in the wilderness, that we would refuse to be overtaken and/or overwhelmed, that we are able to breathe in the good of life and exhale the bad of life daily, that we will not allow ourselves to be so exhausted that we can't call His name. JESUS, I NEED YOU. **(Hebrews 4:16) "Let us there-**

fore come boldly unto the throne of grace, that we may obtain mercy, and find grace to help in time of need."

All things are but a process. This process, our process, will lead us closer to the presence and love of our Father.

I pray: that we would climb into our Father's arms and welcome Him to love us, that we would rest and put our complete trust in Him, that we would receive our security in His arms, that we will allow our ears to rest upon His heart and as we lie in His arms, that we would wrap ourselves in His love and divine favor, that we will be strong and not weak, that we would live and not die, that we would fight and not faint, that when life sends trials and distresses, we would go into that quiet place in our mind and heart where we meet Him only to cast our cares and allow ourselves to empty the pain and take on the pleasure of merely being in His presence. To God be the Glory!

Additional References: Philippians 4:19, Isaiah. 25:4,1Chronicles. 28:9, 1John 4:16

Reflections:

His Love

All praises to the God we serve. I am a vessel being used to pray and encourage you and I thank God and follow in the way in which He wants me to go daily giving Him all the Glory.

I'm thankful for the words God gives me. As the eagle that I am, I fly alone. I soar in the wind of God's breath that He breathes upon me. He fuels me. He motivates me. When I face obstacles, He whispers encouragement in my ears. He is the lover of my soul.

Oh what a feeling it is to finally find someone whose love is not predicated upon what I do but who I am. I am HIS. **(Ps. 9: 1-2) "I will praise thee, O LORD, with my whole heart; I will tell of all your wonders. I will be glad and rejoice in thee: I will sing praise to thy name, O thou most High."**

I pray: that we would allow God to be the center and the focal point of our life, allow Him to be the lover of our soul, that in His presence we find safety, calm, peace, joy and love that surpasses our understanding, that wisdom be served and our life preserved, that our fears would be erased and replaced with our dreams, that we sit as hungry humble servants bowing down at His feet, that we would look up and never look down, that we allow Him to kiss our tears away, that we would allow Him to hold us in His arms and rock us in His divine purpose.**(Job 41:22) "In his neck remaineth strength, and sorrow is turned into joy before him"**

He is so in love with us that He has given us a will to take what He's offering or leave it. He is so in love with us that no one can do anything to us that He doesn't allow, and He allows it so that it will make us run to Him. He wants us so bad that He allows things to happen just so that He can comfort us and brings us to a better understanding of His grace mercy and love - who He is.

I pray for a greater understanding of God's love for all of us. To God be The Glory!

Additional References: Ps.13:2, Proverbs 10:22, Isaiah 51:11, John 7:37, James 4:8, Ps.145:20, 1Corinthians 8:3

Reflections:

Escape the Snares of the Devil

⟨⟨⟩⟩

What a Mighty, Merciful, Loving Father we have. Praise Him for He is worthy. He is ultimate. He is gracious and faithful.

Death traps were set for me, but I am still here because my Father has a plan for me ooh but my plan took me so far away from the Father into a world of pain and tribulation, but when I called God, when I cried for help, He heard me and delivered me out of all my afflictions. From His throne, from the heavenly places He heard me and continues to hear all of our cries. **(Ps.103: 1-5) "Bless the LORD, O my soul: and all that is within me, bless his holy name. Bless the LORD, O my soul, and forget not all his benefits: Who forgiveth all thine iniquities; who healeth all thy diseases; Who redeemeth thy life from destruction; who crowneth thee with lovingkindness and tender mercies; Who satisfieth thy mouth with good things; so that thy youth is renewed like the eagle's."**

I pray: that we will continue to cry out to Him it is our cry that brings us right into His presence, that we rest in His presence because it is in His presence where we can find rest from the things of this world, it is in His presence that He attends to our every need. He makes us feel like we have Him all to ourselves, so we must give Him all of us. He is our escape. We must give Him even those areas that we have been trying to hold on to because they have been our security.

I pray that we will never be surprised to be loved, God knew us before we were formed in our mother's womb. He can make our life complete when we place all the pieces of our broken hearts and our discouraged minds before Him. God can give us a fresh start. **(Jeremiah 24:7) "And I will give them an heart to know me, that I am the LORD: and they shall be my people, and I will be their God: for they shall return unto me with their whole heart."**

I pray that everyday we review His works, we take in to account all that He has done for us before we even called Him Savior, that we would be alert to all His ways. He has the ability to put us back together and keep us. God can rewrite what was written if we open the book of our heart. God has given us a fresh start; stop reviewing the past and live daily refreshed by His love and presence. In all things PRAISE HIM!!! To God Be The Glory!

Additional References: Jeremiah 32:41, Matthew 9:22, Colossians 2:6-7, Philippians 4:7, James 4:8

Reflections:

Let Us All Pray

❧

Pray with me knowing that we are asking for change, change that may not always feel good to our flesh.

*F*ather God, we come to You in the mighty name of Jesus seeking Your face asking for You to help us to remove ourselves and seek more of You. We are touching and agreeing in Spirit and You said that if two or three are joined together in agreement You would hear and give us whatever it is that we ask in line with Your will. **(Ps.119:169) "Let my cry come near before thee, O Lord: give me understanding according to thy word."**

We ask that You give us more of You and less of us. We ask You to take complete control of our lives. We ask that You guide us, protect us, and give us all knowledge needed to accomplish Your will in our life. God we ask You to live inside of us show us our secret sin and protect us from all anxiety. God we ask that You direct our steps and give us clarity on the steps You have for our future. We ask You to deliver our spouse to us, for those of us who are single and have a desire to be married.

We pray for our spouse right now that You also direct their steps to us and that You prepare us to receive them when they arrive.

For those of us who are married we ask You to make us

brides not just wives. We ask You to help us love our husbands as You expect us to. We ask You to show us how to be better brides. We accept all things from You and our greatest desire is to do Your will.

Father, for those of us who are men and reading these words, we ask You to make them line up with Your will, and teach them how to love their wives as Christ loves the church. For those who are yet married, Lord prepare them to be priests. We ask that if anything in us is lacking that you show us what to do to ensure that we are completely prepared for what You have for us.

God be good to us on this day. We give You all the sacrifices of praise. We honor and adore You and we know that it is You above all others that can give us the desires of our heart.

We thank You, and in the name of Jesus, we count all that was asked in this prayer done. We cover ourselves with the blood of Jesus and we love You, thank You, praise You, lift You up, glorify You, magnify You, because You are worthy of OUR ALL Amen! To God be the Glory!

Reflections:

Acceptance

*G*od is good. I worship Him for all that He is and praise Him for all that He has been. All praises to the lifter of my head. He is faithful. He is a mighty God.

God eternally loved His son and He eternally loves us. Jesus suffered for us and for that He is worthy of our love and obedience. We cannot let it be hard to forgive ourselves because that is the devil. He makes us think that what we have done is really worse than it really is.

Nothing is bigger than God if we repent. We have to ask for forgiveness ,and every time the devil brings it back to our memory we have to tell him that we have already been forgiven and we are not going to give that subject any more place in our mind. **(Ps.138:1) "I will praise thee with my whole heart: before the gods will I sing praise unto thee."**

I pray: that we understand our worth, our beauty inside and out, our intelligence, and all the gifts God has given us to do His purpose. I pray: that we prove to the devil that he is a liar and that he has no place in our mind, that we accept God's grace and Mercy that will continue to bring us through, that God gives us a greater revelation of who He knows we are and we stop acting on who we think we are. We have a forgiving Father, a Father that said I will **(Hebrews13:5) "never leave you or forsake you." (Ps. 103: 2-3) "Bless the LORD, O my soul, and forget not all his benefits: Who forgiveth all thine iniquities; who**

healeth all thy diseases;"

We could never withstand punishment from God. Although the devil doesn't want us to get a hold of that revelation because if we understand and receive this we would be FREE. FREE from the lies of the devil. We are redeemed by Jesus and delivered by His divine power. **(Malachi 4:2-3) "But unto you that fear my name shall the Sun of righteousness arise with healing in his wings; and ye shall go forth, and grow up as calves of the stall. And ye shall tread down the wicked; for they shall be ashes under the soles of your feet in the day that I shall do this, saith the LORD of hosts."** To God be the GLORY!

<u>**Additional References**</u>: 1John 4:16, Romans 8:17-19, Hebrews 12:6-8, 1Timothy 4:8

<u>**Reflections:**</u>

Grace

I lift my hands praising a worthy God and distracting a busy devil. I open my mouth and let praise fill this room. I sing songs of thanksgiving because I know who I am in the eyes of my Father.

I thank Him for creating me exactly like He wanted me to be. Praise His Holy name because He is great and greatly we shall praise Him. **(Ps.150:6) "Let everything that hath breath praise the Lord. Praise ye the Lord."**

I thank Him for His grace that is new to me every morning. Grace wouldn't let us go our own way. Grace blocks our path to possible destruction. We've seen people lose their minds and be destroyed going through the same things we went through. GRACE SAVED US. **(Genesis 19:19) "Behold now, thy servant hath found grace in thy sight, and thou hast magnified thy mercy, which thou hast shewed unto me in saving my life."** That's why GRACE is AMAZING. GRACE is directed by supreme intelligence. GRACE is not directed towards you because you love GOD, but because of supreme intelligence what GOD decides.

(Genesis 34:11) "And Shechem said unto her father and unto her brethren, let me find grace in your eyes, and what ye shall say unto me I will give." (Exodus 33:13) "Now therefore, I pray thee, if I have found grace in thy sight." (John 1: 16) "And of his fullness have all we received, and grace for grace."

We reach for things, pray for things and don't get it, that's GRACE intervening for what we don't need. Everything works together for the GOOD for those who love the LORD. Your heartbreak - GRACE, Your disappointment - GRACE, Your loss -GRACE. So I pray that if you have to lose some things to be BLESSED - LOSE THEM, that if you have to be removed from some things - be removed. TO GOD BE THE GLORY!!

Additional References: John14:26, Ps.3, James 4:6, Acts4:33

Reflections:

In His Arms

What a mighty God we serve. God is GOOD. God is a God of a second chance. He is faithful and He is just. He has a plan and a purpose for my life and I'm thankful. I thank Him for the choices that He has made for me. I love Him more than life because He is my life. He is all that I need and everything that I want. He is the lover of my soul. He is the air that I breathe and I'm thankful that He breathes love into me daily. **(Ps. 47: 1-2,6) "O clap your hands, all ye people; shout unto God with the voice of triumph. For the LORD most high is terrible; he is a great King over all the earth. Sing praises to God, sing praises: sing praises unto our King, sing praises."**

I pray: that we will confidently know where to run to when the tests of life seem to be overwhelming, that we know where to go when we feel like giving up, when we feel like everything we need we can't reach. BUT GOD! God is so awesome because He has offered us His hand, His arms and His heart. We can sit in His loving arms and ask Him to wrap His love around us and keep us. He will keep us in His nest when we are weak and prepare us to get ready to fly again. When we are weak within ourselves, we are strong and mighty in Him. We can look to the hills where our help comes from. If God be for us who shall be against us.

I pray: that we will be encouraged in Him whenever we need to be, that after we have cried and felt like giving up that we will walk if we need to and run if we have to into the arms of the Father who said I WILL NEVER LEAVE YOU OR FORSAKE YOU.

(Ps. 21:1-6) **"The king shall joy in thy strength, O LORD; and in thy salvation how greatly shall he rejoice! Thou hast given him his heart's desire, and hast not withholden the request of his lips. Selah. For thou preventest him with the blessings of goodness: thou settest a crown of pure gold on his head. He asked life of thee, and thou gavest it him, even length of days for ever and ever. His glory is great in thy salvation: honour and majesty hast thou laid upon him. For thou hast made him most blessed for ever: thou hast made him exceeding glad with thy countenance."**

God does not expect us to be perfect, but He expects that we will allow Him to per fect us. When we are weak, He is strong. To God be the Glory!

Additional References: Deuteronomy 33:27, Exodus33:15, Ps.16:11, Acts 3:19, Ladies- a must have book suggestion: The Lady, The Lover, The Lord by T.D. Jakes

Reflections:

We are Here to be Built

〰️

T praise Him! I worship Him! I glorify Him! I thank Him! I receive His grace and mercy! I give Him all the GLORY. I am what I am because of my wonderful FATHER. He created me Great! He molded me perfect!

I am what I am because this is exactly what He wants me to be. I am obedient to His call. I am attentive to His voice, and I am a vessel to be used. I'm thankful to Him for using me to do His will.

I'm thankful that daily He strengthens me to be all that He has predestined me to be. I love Him! I adore Him and I rest in Him knowing that my God, my Father, my Lover, my Comforter is always there when I need Him and when He is quiet I still know His peace rests deep down inside of me. He is great and greatly I will praise Him. **(Ps. 64: 10) "The righteous shall be glad in the LORD, and shall trust in him; and all the upright in heart shall glory."**

We go through life and it is not always easy. Some things won't always make sense to our fleshly eye. It may get really hard and we feel like giving up. BUT GOD - The supplier of our every need. If we are obedient, patient, willing and focused on Him, He will give us the peace that we need to withstand any and everything.

God will never give us more than we can handle. He will give us all that we need to accomplish what He has predestined for us to do. Things will not always be hard; sometimes things will also come easy. We will be blessed above and beyond anything that we could ever ask for. It won't even make sense to our fleshly eye. People will give us things who owe us nothing. Everything we need is in His presence.

I pray today that: **(Proverbs 3: 5-6)** **"Trust in the LORD with all thine heart; and lean not unto thine own understanding. In all thy ways acknowledge him, and he shall direct thy paths." (Proverbs 14:1) "Every wise woman buildeth her house: but the foolish plucketh it down with her hands."**

I pray: that we will be wise and build up our house (body, mind and spirit), that we would build our house up by filling it with the word of the God who has given us promises of healing, prosperity, strength, unconditional love, grace and mercy, that we would allow God to bring out the best in us by putting the best in us through His direction, that we would have a heart of peace. **(Proverbs 14:30) "A heart of peace gives life to the body."** I speak peace into our hearts that nothing stands in the way of God's will in our life not even US. To God be The GLORY!

Additional References: Nehemiah 8:10, Ps.37:4, Hebrews11:6, Ps.90:1, Hebrews11:10, Philippians 4:7

Reflections:

I Adore Him

*T*his is the day that the Lord has made I choose to rejoice and be glad in it. It's a new season, a new day. I bless Him because of who He is to me, lover of my soul, the love of my heart, my provider, my strong tower, my deliver, my first husband, my best friend, my father and my mother. He is all things to me and in all things I lift up my hands to praise a God who has given me an identity. I have a love life. God has given me vision and through that vision I speak. **(Ps.104: 1) "Bless the LORD, O my soul. O LORD my God, thou art very great; thou art clothed with honor and majesty."**

I pray: that God would equip us to serve Him, that He would equip us to give through us but from Him, that God would teach us how to give based on Him and when we get hurt we go to Him for healing.

God wants us to show people Him. Sometimes we will be required to go out and help the hurting. Hurt people - hurt people. So, there will be times when we will get hurt doing the service of the Lord. It is then that we retrieve back into the loving arms of our Father to be healed and refilled. It is then that we draw close to Him when the pain gets overwhelming, when it comes from a unexpected source.

God will strengthen us to give even when it doesn't seem fair. God will strengthen us so that no matter what we think or feel that we remain obedient to Him, because if we do what God wants us to do regardless of what we feel, He will always fill us back up. We give so that He can give us back. He wants us to be empty because He is a jealous God.

A God that wants us to come to a place that EVERY-THING we need is in His presence and we are not just there taking it because it's being offered, we are there taking it because we need it.

I need Him more than anything in this world. I need Him. I need Him to wake me up in the morning and wrap His arms around me and tell me that I'm not alone. I need Him to ride in my car with me and listen to my morning praises to Him. I need Him to walk into work with me so that He can show me the beauty of His sunlight and make me feel, even if it's 20 degrees out, like it's 80 because His warmth warms me up. I need Him to sit with me all day at work so that when people get on my nerves I don't step inside myself and deal with them, but I stay in Him.

I don't know about you, but every moment of the day, I need Him and I pray that every moment of the day you realize that you have Him because He will stand there quiet until we call Him and then He'll give us all of Him all that we ask for and it'll be more than what we thought we needed. TO GOD BE THE GLORY!!!!!!

Additional References: Acts 3:19, Proverbs 3:6, Luke 12:30, Philippians 4:12

Reflections:

Love

*G*od is good all the time. I thank Him for His love that keeps me. I thank Him that I can draw close to Him and feel Him.

I praise Him because I know that if it had not been for Him I would not be here. I weep tears of joy realizing that the love I need the most, the kind of love I desire to have, and the unconditional love that I am able to receive, I have above and beyond anything that I could ever imagine from my best friend, the lover of my soul, the comforter of my heart and the embrace of my daddy-God.

What a friend I have in Jesus. I'm thankful today that I have LOVE. A human, not man or a woman can match God's love. Love that is mastered and incomparable to anything I've ever felt. I'm grateful that He looked for me, He found me, and He saved me from myself, from my direction, from my plan. Praise God! **(2Chronicles 7: 3) "And when all the children of Israel saw how the fire came down, and the glory of the LORD upon the house, they bowed themselves with their faces to the ground upon the pavement, and worshipped, and praised the LORD, saying, For he is good; for his LOVE endureth for ever."**

I pray: that we sit right in this moment and allow God to whisper sweet everything in our ear, that we sit and wrap our arms around our self and ask Him to come and sit with us and allow His presence to squeeze us so tight that we lose our breath, so that at this point He can breathe His breath into us, that we lose our self in Him, that we would let Him take our breath away, that once we have inhaled His breath we can exhale the breath of disappointment, of loneliness, of heartbreak, of unforgiveness, of DEATH, that the next breath we inhale will be a breath of courage, faith, excitement, wholeness, love and LIFE. When we know what it feels like to be loved, we will be drawn to it.

I pray: that as we are drawn to GODLY love we will be drawn to GODLY people, that after we have received the best from God, we will have a greater expectation of what love SHOULD look like. Once we've learned to freely receive, we will know how to freely give and when we are hurt in this process we understand that what we are giving is of God, not of us and we will endure pain less. Jesus said we can forgive because we realize that we must forgive them because they know not what they do.

I pray that we will become so mature through the love of Christ that we can love people in spite of themselves, loving them as God loves us. God is LOVE and because He is...

I pray: that we allow Him to use us as a vessel to give what He wants every person that comes in contact with us exactly what we have been prepared and predestined to give them, leaving what we think and feel out of it, that we would look, in all people, for GOD, and that people would look in us for Him because He is here. It is better to give than it is to receive.

(1John 3: 23) "And this is his commandment, That we should believe on the name of his Son Jesus Christ, and love one another, as he gave us commandment." (1John 4: 16-18) "And we have known and believed the love that God hath to us. God is love; and he that dwelleth in love dwelleth in God, and God in him. Herein is our love made perfect, that we may have boldness in the day of judgment: because as he is, so are we in this world. There is no fear in love; but perfect love casteth out fear: because fear hath torment. He that feareth is not made perfect in love." To God Be The GLORY!

Additional References: 1John 4:12, Song of Songs 8:6, John 13:35, Romans 13:10, 1Corinthians 13:13, book suggestion: Reduce me to love by Joyce Meyer

Reflections:

God, I Need:

You to release the power of Your word in my life
You when I am weak to be strong
You to always see my heart
You to love me in spite of myself
You to develop me
Your word to spiritually nourish me
that I might fulfill my purpose
You in every area of my life
You to allow Your word to penetrate in me
You to cleanse my mind
You from moment to moment
You to conform me, make me more like Christ
You to mold me in the likeness of Christ
You to use Your word to infuse hope in me
You to never leave me
You to give me more and more joy daily
Your word to heal me of my past and present hurts
You to be strong when I am weak
You to show me what I need to learn
You to help me be the best I can be
You to use me for Your Glory
You to help me to grow and mature
that I might be more like Christ
You to help me grow up and not give up
Your word to build character in me
You that I may be strengthened
You to go before me
You to spiritually give me strength for the journey
You to keep me in my time of loneliness
You to bless me
You to enlarge my territory
Your word to produce change in my life
You to show me Your will and Your way for my life

I totally focus on my ultimate goal in life to passionately know Your will and Your way

Let Us All Pray

Pray with me knowing that we are asking for change, change that may not always feel good to our flesh.

Father God,

We come before You praising You, giving You all the Glory and the entire honor. We bless Your holy name. We know that there is no one like You and no one above You. We ask that You would guide us in all our ways.

Lord, teach us to be more like You. We ask that You rest in the hearts of Your people who have been called by name to serve You. We thank You for taking us out of our sin, out of our fleshly ways and building us up to serve You diligently. We ask that You stay close because we recognize that without You we are nothing but in You we are fearfully and wonderfully made, predestined to do great things. We ask You to use us for Your glory.

Teach us to be more humble, teach us the way in which You want us to go, guide our steps, direct our paths, and strengthen us for the journey of life in which You have us on. We love and adore You and recognize You in every area in our lives. You are LORD. We rest in Your holiness and we receive all of Your grace.

Lord, be Lord over every area of our lives, teach us to

love as You love. We want to be in perfect line with Your will. We want the desires of our heart but we want those desires to be deposited in our heart by You.

We submit to Your will and to Your way. We love You and thank You for never leaving us or forsaking us even when we deserved to be deserted. We don't see You as man because man will always fail, but we look at You as GOD.

The God who cannot lie, the God whose promises are YES and AMEN. We praise You Lord not only for what You have done, but also for who You are. Your presence is comfort, Your voice is soothing and Your direction is clear. We love You Lord, our refuge, our strength, our ever-present help, our love and our Father. AMEN

Reflections:

Faith

*H*e is so amazing, so incredible, so above and beyond all that in this life I could ever think I could have. He is the lover of my soul, the creator of a wonderful people, people who desire to love Him and be in His presence.

I thank Him for His grace and mercy that is new to me every morning. I thank Him for loving me above and beyond anything I could ever ask for. I thank Him for His faithfulness. **(Exodus 15:1-2)" Then sang Moses and the children of Israel this song unto the LORD, and spake, saying, I will sing unto the LORD, for he hath triumphed gloriously: the horse and his rider hath he thrown into the sea. The LORD is my strength and song, and he is become my salvation: he is my God, and I will prepare him an habitation; my father's God, and I will exalt him."**

I pray: that we will believe and have faith daily that He will always keep us in all of our circumstances, that our faith will increase daily, that we will draw close to Him and allow Him to keep us, that we have a permanent love affair with the ultimate lover.

(Hebrews 11:6) "But without faith it is impossible to please him: for he that cometh to God must believe that he is, and that he is a rewarder of them that diligently seek him." (James 1: 6-8) "But let him ask in faith, nothing wavering. For he that wavereth is like a wave of the sea driven with the wind and tossed. For let not that man

think that he shall receive any thing of the Lord. A double minded man is unstable in all his ways." (Hebrews 4:2) "For unto us was the gospel preached, as well as unto them: but the word preached did not profit them, not being mixed with faith in them that heard it. " (Proverbs 3: 5) "Trust in the Lord with all your heart, and lean not onto thine own understanding." (James 1:2-3) "My brethren, count it all joy when ye fall into divers temptations; Knowing this, that the trying of your faith worketh patience."

I pray that we will have faith beyond measure, joy beyond comprehension, trust beyond our circumstances, love beyond understanding and peace beyond time. TO GOD BE THE GLORY!

Additional References: Galatians 3:2, 2:20, Ephesians 3:12, Titus 1:1, Romans 12:3

Reflections:

Give Thanks to the Lord

~~~

He is marvelous. He is great and greatly I will praise Him. I honor Him and love Him today.

(Ps. 136: 1-5,12) "Give thanks to the Lord, for He is good. His love endures forever. Give thanks to the God of gods. His love endures forever. Give thanks to the Lord of lords: His love endures forever. To Him alone do my praises go up, He alone does great wonders, His love endures forever. Who by His understanding made the heavens, His love endures forever. With mighty hands and outstretched arms; His love endures forever"

(Ps. 139: 1-12) "O LORD, thou hast searched me, and known me. Thou knowest my downsitting and mine uprising, thou understandest my thought afar off. Thou compassest my path and my lying down, and art acquainted with all my ways. For there is not a word in my tongue, but, lo, O LORD, thou knowest it altogether. Thou hast beset me behind and before, and laid thine hand upon me. Such knowledge is too wonderful for me; it is high, I cannot attain unto it. Whither shall I go from thy spirit? or whither shall I flee from thy presence? If I ascend up into heaven, thou art there: if I make my bed in hell, behold, thou art there. If I take the wings of the morning, and dwell in the uttermost parts of the sea;

Even there shall thy hand lead me, and thy right hand shall hold me. If I say, Surely the darkness shall cover me; even the night shall be light about me. Yea, the darkness hideth not from thee; but the night shineth as the day: the darkness and the light are both alike to thee."

I pray that we will be still and know that we serve a God that will meet us where we are. A God that will keep us, Even when we go to the dark places in our life He will be there to show us that we belong to Him, to show us that His love endures forever and He will be the light in the midst of our darkness. I pray that we will read this and absorb this word, let it rule richly in your heart. Get this in your spirit. To God Be The Glory!!!!!!!!!!

Additional References: Ephesians 5:20, 1Thessalonians 3:9, Revelation 4:9

Reflections:

Hear Him

*P*raise the Lord, Praise the God who loves, Praise the God who restores, refines, relieves and rejuvenates. He's excellent, how excellent is His name. He's great and wonderful and I thank Him for His grace and mercy. **(Ps. 8:1) "O Lord our Lord, how excellent is thy name in all the earth! Who hast set thy glory above the heavens."**

Every morning I wake up and there is that one moment of extreme aloneness, when I go from sleep to awareness. In that moment there is stillness, it is in this moment before I realize anything else that I open my ears to hear my Father speak to me. To hear the lover of our soul "Say Something." It is that moment that we should listen for God. That is when we hear Him whisper sweet everything in our ear. He will start our day off with "I love you and I promise to keep you today. I promise to comfort you when you need it. Show my love to you when you desire it. Take control when you ask for it."

I pray today: that we know God's word. **(Romans 8: 31) "What shall we then say to these things? If God be for us, who can be against us?" (Ps. 1: 6) "For the LORD knoweth the way of the righteous: but the way of the ungodly shall perish."**

I pray that we would know His voice and draw to Him when we need to hear Him speak to us, not just in the morning, but in all that we do daily. Whatever we need He can guide us.

I pray that, as we confidently know His ways and His company, that we will remain in His peace and love. To God be the GLORY!!!

Additional References: Ephesians 5:19, 2Timothy 1:12, Revelation 2:2, Ps.68:35, John14:12-14, Matthew 17:20

Reflections:

What Are You Using Your Senses For?

$\sim$

I get joy thinking about what GOD has done for me and what He continues to do on my behalf. I worship my faithful Father. I thank Him for wrapping His loving arms around me and loving me from the inside out. **(Exodus 15:2) "The LORD is my strength and song, and he is become my salvation: he is my God, and I will prepare him an habitation; my father's God, and I will exalt him."**

I pray that: we realize that there are things that sit between our head (thinking mind) and our heart (emotions). OUR MOUTH - OUR MOUTH the mouth that God gave us to rebuke the devil, OUR MOUTH that God gave us to proclaim His word, OUR MOUTH that God gave us to speak into existence His promises, that we would use OUR MOUTH in the way that God wants us to, that we use it when we fall in between, thinking (mind) our self into depression or feeling (heart) our way into sadness.

I pray that: we realize that OUR EARS sit between our mind and our heart, they are there so that we can listen to our Father tell us He loves us, that He'll never leave us or forsake us, that we would tune OUR EARS out of listening to the devil who attacks our mind and makes us think the opposite of God's word, that we would tune OUR EARS out of listening to our heart tell us about the things we lost and how much we need to be loved when God has already told us everything we need is in HIS presence.

I pray: that we realize that OUR EYES sit between our mind and heart. OUR EYES that God has given us to see what He has done for us, see that home that we have, those children, that car, that job. See what He has given you.

I pray that we would use our eyes to see what He has done and not allow the devil to show us all the things that He hasn't. See that God will give you the desires of your heart in His perfect timing. We should use our mouth to speak, use our ears to hear, use our eyes to see, and when we feel like we can't speak, hear, or see remember that the distance between our head and our knees is much longer with a lot of things in between that can help or hinder us, but the distance between our knees and the floor is a lot shorter.

So, try GOD! Get on your knees and show Him that you hunger for His presence. Then let Him stand you back up and give you the strength/maturity to use the things that He has given to you. When we've done all we can we have to stand, but when we can't stand, kneel, and when we can't kneel, lay flat on our face and seek the presence of the God whose promises are Yes and AMEN! To GOD Be The Glory!

Additional References: Isaiah.55:3, Habakkak 2:4, Ps.119:132, 2Corinthians 3:18, Ephesians 3:17-19

Reflections:

The Will of God

⁓

*P*raise Him in the morning, praise Him in the afternoon, and praise Him when the sun goes down. I praise Him because I have no other choice when I look at the things that He has done.

When I look at where I came from and faithfully believe that He has plans to take me further than I have ever imagined, I MUST praise Him.

I praise Him because of the thought of where I could be or where I would of been had it not been for Him on my side. It is these thoughts that give me fuel to praise, that give me energy to praise His mighty name. It is a wonderful feeling to be in God's will. **(Ps. 20:5) "We will rejoice in Thy salvation."**

I pray: that God would SHOW us His will for our lives or HELP us to be patient as He brings to pass all that He has promised, that we WALK a walk of confidence, that we SEE Him in everything we do and the things that we don't see Him in, we remove our self from, that we WELCOME more of Him and less of us, that everything we need we FIND in His presence, that this day we receive all that He has in His plan for us, that we REALIZE that He chose us before the foundation of the world to be Holy and blameless before Him in love, that we UNDERSTAND He predestined us to be His precious children because it was His greatest pleasure to do so, and that we RECEIVE His tremendous Grace toward us. He made us accepted in the beloved, no longer desperate for love or devastated at the rejection of people, but fulfilled and contented in Him. To GOD Be The Glory!

Additional References: Jonah 1:6, Micah 6:8, 1Corinthians 14:25, Philippians1:6, Colossians 1:10

Reflections:

He Wants to Use US

*P*raise the Lord, Praise Him. Glorify His name. He is worthy! Honor Him! Give Him exalted praise. He is awesome and wonderful. He is faithful and just. He is mighty in battle and He is our God, Our Father, and our Lord. God is worthy!

He is worthy to be magnified and glorified. He is faithful and in all things I adore Him. **(Ps.103:1-2) "Praise the Lord, O my soul: all my inmost being, praise his holy name. Praise the Lord, O my soul and forget not all his benefits."**

God's plan is perfect and it is His plan for us to read these words at this time, in this moment. It is imperative that we recognize where our Father is and where He isn't. God is present to be our direction, to direct our ways and guide our steps. God has planned everything we go through in our lives.

We go through not only for the building of ourselves but also for the building of the many people who are all around us. We go through so that He can use us to bring someone else through a situation that we have already conquered by the grace of God. We go through the storms of life because God has given us the strength and power to overcome them all.

I pray: so deeply that we go through and not give up, that we utilize God to help us in every and anyway that we need Him, that we go through that we might help God, help the hurting, encourage the weak, and to humble our hearts that we might confirm to people that they are not alone in their circumstances. God wants to use us! Think about where we could be!

I pray: **(Ephesians 1:15-19) "Wherefore I also, after I heard of your faith in the Lord Jesus, and love unto all the saints, Cease not to give thanks for you, making mention of you in my prayers; That the God of our Lord Jesus Christ, the Father of glory, may give unto you the spirit of wisdom and revelation in the knowledge of him: The eyes of your understanding being enlightened; that ye may know what is the hope of his calling, and what the riches of the glory of his inheritance in the saints, And what is the exceeding greatness of his power to us-ward who believe, according to the working of his mighty power,"**

I pray also that the eyes of our heart may be enlightened in order that we may know the hope to which He has called us, the riches of His glorious inheritance in the saints, and His incomparably great power for us who believe. That power is like the working of His mighty strength. VICTORY IS OURS! TO GOD BE THE GLORY!

Additional References: 2Corinthians 10:5, Proverbs 1:23, 29:18, Ps.144:1-2

Reflections:

Let us Pray

Prepare your hearts for prayer, clear your minds for purity, and rest in this moment knowing that the next one will be a moment of expectancy for greatness to evolve.

Father God, we come to You in the mighty name of Jesus seeking Your face asking for You to help us to remove ourselves and seek more of You. We come before You Father with humble hearts and open ears. We recognize You as Lord and Savior over our lives.

We know that it is through You that we have been saved. It is through You that we receive peace that passes all understanding and it is through You that we receive unspeakable joy. We ask Father that You would draw near to us as we draw near to You. We ask that You would be our ever-present help. We give You free reign in our lives. We recognize that there is no one like You.

If there is any eye reading these words whose heart is broken we ask You Father to speak love into that heart right now, wrap Your loving arms around them and give them the healing comfort, be a heart fixer right now God.

Father, if there is any eye that is reading these words that has a need we ask You right now to be a need meeter. Father, if there is any eye that is reading these words that can't find their way we ask God that You would be a way maker. Father, we come to You because we believe and place our trust in You, we come to You because we know that in You there is fullness of joy and it is in You where we confidently know we can be loved.

Love on us Father as we love on You that we might be strengthened and equipped to do Your will not always because we agree with what and how You do things, but because we love You enough and know that You love us enough to know what is best for us. We thank You and praise You. In the mighty name of Jesus! To God be the Glory!

<u>Reflections:</u>

He is Worthy

⤳

*H*e is worthy of all the honor, all the praise, and all the Glory. He is a good GOD. I sit thankful today that when I looked in the mirror this morning I saw a woman in the midst of being perfected for the will of her perfect Father.

A changed woman, a woman that God has changed dramatically to be prepared to do His will. I thank Him that I'm not where I used to be and praise Him while I'm on my way to where He wants me to be. **(Hebrews 13:15-16) "By him therefore let us offer the sacrifice of praise to God continually, that is, the fruit of our lips giving thanks to his name. But to do good and to communicate forget not: for with such sacrifices God is well pleased."**

I pray: that we would look back over our lives and see all that God has brought us through, and as we look, we allow GOD to build patience and compassion in us, that we would use the tools that God has given us as He has built us up, changed us, encouraged us, and loved us, that we would lay on our face in humble submission, sit in perfect peace, stand in all trials, walk through the uncomfortable processes, run in our daily race until we see His face, soar through the storms, and get to a greater level of spiritual maturity through it all. **(Deuteronomy 10:12) "And now, Israel, what doth the LORD thy God require of thee, but to fear the LORD thy God, to walk in all his ways, and to love him, and to serve the LORD thy God with**

all thy heart and with all thy soul" To God be the Glory!

Additional References: 2Timothy 3:7, Matthew 4:9, Luke 4:7, 1Peter 2:24, Romans 5:9

Reflections:

Let Me be the Lamp

*T*sing praises to the most high God, the lover of my
soul, my lily in the valley, my rock and my fortress,
my strong tower, my provider, my best friend. He's all I
need and everything I want, He is the God who gives me
love above and beyond any love ever imagined.

Oh how sweet the words those that leave His lips that
land on my ears and rejuvenate my heart. When I sit and
think about the love affair that I have with a God who I worship, the intimacy that I experience with Him in the midst of
my praise, the marriage that I have sealed with my adoration,
I am willing to be a vessel for Him to use. **(Ps.107: 1,21-22)
"O give thanks unto the LORD, for he is good: for his
mercy endureth forever. Oh that men would praise the
LORD for his goodness, and for his wonderful works to
the children of men! And let them sacrifice the sacrifices
of thanksgiving, and declare his works with rejoicing."**

Ask God to use you in any way that He wants and NO
DEVIL in hell can hinder His plan.

God will help us to see the GOOD that He is doing in us
regardless of what it looks like. He will strengthen us for the
journey of life that He has put us on.

I pray: that if you don't have one, you begin a love affair
with God, that you return to your first love, that you become
a lamp stand to reflect the light of the most HIGH GOD.
(Revelation 21: 23) "And the city had no need of the sun,

neither of the moon, to shine in it: for the glory of God did lighten it, and the Lamb is the light thereof."

In the Bible the lamp represents the presence of God and the light is His word being brought forth. If we are lamp stands where ever we are, so will His presence be and the words that exit our mouths will be of Him because of His powerful presence in us.

I pray: that God will equip us through His love, through intimacy with us, to be His lamp stands, that we will stand for God in all that we say and do so that everyone will see that the light of the world rest in us, so every one around us will witness the glory of God, that they might be encouraged when they look at where God has brought us from and the rays that shine on the outside that God has deposited in the inside. **(Luke 11: 33)** **"No man, when he hath lighted a candle, putteth it in a secret place, neither under a bushel, but on a candlestick, that they which come in may see the light."** To God be the GLORY!

Additional References: Ps.36:9, 97:11, Isaiah 5:20, 1John 6:58, Titus 1:2

Reflections:

Praise Him

(Ps. 40:1- 10) "I waited patiently for the LORD; and he inclined unto me, and heard my cry. He brought me up also out of an horrible pit, out of the miry clay, and set my feet upon a rock, and established my goings. And he hath put a new song in my mouth, even praise unto our God: many shall see it, and fear, and shall trust in the LORD. Blessed is that man that maketh the LORD his trust, and respecteth not the proud, nor such as turn aside to lies. Many, O LORD my God, are thy wonderful works which thou hast done, and thy thoughts which are to us-ward: they cannot be reckoned up in order unto thee: if I would declare and speak of them, they are more than can be numbered. Sacrifice and offering thou didst not desire; mine ears hast thou opened: burnt offering and sin offering hast thou not required. Then said I, Lo, I come: in the volume of the book it is written of me, I delight to do thy will, O my God: yea, thy law is within my heart. I have preached righteousness in the great congregation: lo, I have not refrained my lips, O LORD, thou knowest. I have not hid thy righteousness within my heart; I have declared thy faithfulness and thy salvation: I have not concealed thy lovingkindness and thy truth from the great congregation."

God is a good God.

I pray that we will let these Psalms speak for us in many ways, let us be thankful for where God has brought us from and where He is taking us to, let us be thankful that when we call Him He hears our cry, even when we feel out of place and undeserving of His love, let us praise Him.

I pray that we will wait patiently for Him. Some of us met God when we hit our bottom, when we reached the place where all we could do was fall on our knees because we were so broken.

Some of us met God when we went through a series of pain that nothing or no one could heal us, although we tried many things, but it was God who whispered, "Come near to me." Some of us have been in the church all of our lives and it wasn't until the church disappointed us so many times that we realized who God was. Aren't you glad you met Him -Well tell Him! Praise HIM! Praise Him! Praise the Lord EVERYBODY! No matter where you met Him, no matter what you've come through, God's plan is perfect and He is available. He is our ever-present Help. To GOD BE THE GLORY!

Additional References: Ephesians 5:19-20, Deuteronomy 10:21, Judges 5:3, Ps.7:17

Reflections:

Intimately Praise Him

What a wonderful day it is. All praises due to the God we serve. I will bless the Lord at all times and His praises shall continually be in my mouth. Praise God for all that He has done and all that He has promised to do. He is worthy. He is marvelous and worthy to be praised.

I honor Him right now. I thank Him for the anointing that He has placed on my life. I thank Him for being a heart fixer and a way maker. I thank Him that He has deemed me worthy to do His perfect work. I thank Him for breaking the bondage off of my life. FREEDOM is so wonderful. **(Ps. 100:1-3) "Make a joyful noise unto the LORD, all ye lands. Serve the LORD with gladness: come before his presence with singing. Know ye that the LORD he is God: it is he that hath made us, and not we ourselves; we are his people, and the sheep of his pasture."**

God has made us beautifully and wonderfully. God is our way maker and heart fixer. God has delivered us from ourselves. God gives us the endurance to run the race. God offers light in the midst of darkness. God offers power to the weak. God offers counsel to the ignorant. God takes His place as the lover of our soul. I pray that with this God we will be intimate within our praise.

Through this intimacy with Him we have the opportunity to show Him tell Him that He is worthy, that we love and adore Him, that He is awesome and wonderful, that there is no one greater than Him, that He is our peace and our joy, that we love Him and want to be next to Him that He might breathe on us. Breathe His love, strength, peace and joy into us.

I pray: that we would lift our hands and worship Him, let us magnify Him, that we would thank Him for all that He is and all that He has made us, that we would not GLORIFY our own flesh, but that we would see in every area of our lives that God is the author and the finisher.

Let us not lose focus and not allow God to be glorified in every area of our life. From our inner beauty, to our outer beauty, from our intelligence, to our wisdom, to our love, to our accomplishments, to our sanity, BE GLORIFIED! Be Glorified Lord. We refuse to rob You of the credit You so rightly deserve. We give it Lord because we recognize You as Lord.

I pray that we would intimately praise Him and draw to Him that He might know how important He is in every area of our lives. TO GOD BE THE GLORY!

Additional References: Ps.30:9, Ps.63:3, Isaiah 38:19

Reflections:

Let us Become

*T*his is the day that the Lord has made I choose to rejoice and be glad. I magnify the Lord! He is worthy to be praised. Great is His faithfulness. I will bless the Lord at all times and His praises shall continually be in my mouth. I'm thankful that I have found a place in Him, a place to glorify, magnify and edify my soul. My soul says yes to all His requests.

I'm thankful that I serve a GOD bigger than my finances, bigger than my circumstances, bigger than my trials, bigger than my tribulations. He is worthy to be praised. At all times I will GLORIFY the Lord because it is Him who is worthy to be praised for my accomplishments in life. How wonderful it is to let the light of the Lord shine through me.

It is a light shining so bright that if you don't know Him you are unable to bear the glare, but if you know Him you recognize the shine. He is Holy ooh so Holy. It is my privilege and my honor to worship Him.

I adore Him because there is no one like Him. I honor Him and worship Him for who He has been. Greatly I will give Him great praise. **(Exodus 15:11) "Who is like unto thee, O LORD, among the gods? who is like thee, glorious in holiness, fearful in praises, doing wonders? "**

I pray that we become **(Ephesians 4:1-7) "I therefore, the prisoner of the Lord, beseech you that ye walk worthy of the vocation wherewith ye were called. With all**

lowliness and meekness, with longsuffering, forbearing one another in love; Endeavouring to keep the unity of the Spirit in the bond of peace. There is one body, and one Spirit, even as ye are called in one hope of your calling; One Lord, one faith, one baptism, One God and Father of all, who is above all, and through all, and in you all. But unto every one of us is given grace according to the measure of the gift of Christ."

I pray that we become women of valor, men that can pray and spiritually lead their homes, women who can submit, men who can speak life, women who can birth life, people who can pray, people who walk in their anointing, people with grace, people of appreciation, people who have a spiritual relationship with our Lord, people who plant seeds, and worshipers that continue to grow intimately in God.

I pray: that we would find our place, that we would know what area in life God expects us to work in, within and with others. To God be the Glory!

Additional References: 2Corinthians 3:18,10:12, Colossians 3:23, Ephesians5,Philippians1:6

Reflections:

He Can Meet Our Needs

*O*OH how I love Jesus. He is the best thing that has ever happened to me. He has proven Himself to be all that I need. He is a way maker and a heart fixer. He is my ever - present help, He is a bridge over troubled waters. I present myself as a living sacrifice, my mind, body and mouth to be used by Him, to do His perfect will for my life in spite of. He has done so much for me that If I had ten thousand years I couldn't repay Him so I sit humbly before Him heeding my flesh that He might be glorified in all that I say and do. Praise the name that is above every name.

He always: provides for me, walks with me, talks with me, strengthens me, encourages me and loves us more than and better than any earthly person could attempt to try. I love and adore Him. **(Ps. 47:1-2) "Oh clap your hands, all ye peoples; Shout unto God with the voice of triumph. For Jehovah Most High is terrible; He is a great King over all the earth."**

I pray that we will recognize, focus on, and get tunnel vision for the one who wants to be our ultimate lover, who wants us to draw close to Him in all our ways. The one who desires to be with us every moment of the day.

I pray that God would be the center of our joy, the place in which we find all that we need. God has promised us many things and in all our circumstances.

I pray that we draw close to His promises. God is a need

meeter. He restores, resurrects and revitalizes us. He is all we need, but we must draw close to Him because in Him is the fullness of joy, the peace that passes all understanding, the unspeakable comfort and the unconditional love.

I pray: that we would draw near to Him to love on Him, that we would draw near to Him to receive what we need that we might be prepared for what He has called us to do without wavering, giving up, or getting weary. He is our strength when we get weak. He is the supplier of all that we need. To God be the Glory!

Additional References: Ephesians 2:6, Romans 12:2, 1Kings 8:56, Ps.21:2, 37:4, 50:15, Isaiah 65:24

Reflections:

Let Us Pray

Prepare your hearts for prayer, clear your minds for purity, and rest in this moment knowing that the next one will be a moment of expectancy for greatness to evolve.

Heavenly Father, You have done so many things in our life and we come before You faithful and in awe of Your greatness. We are no longer amazed at how good You are. We glorify You for being so good to us. We thank You for continuing to be faithful to us even when we fall short, we thank You for remaining faithful to the sometimes faithless.

There are moments that we feel like You can't hear us, when we feel like we call on You and You say nothing. Lord, help us not to get too discouraged when we don't hear from You. Help us to see Your presence in the midst of every one of our circumstances. Help us to keep a purposeful heart, a clean heart, and a right spirit.

We thank You that when You make the commission, You make the provision that we may confidently do whatever You have willed for us to do. Help us to remember the great things that You have predestined us to do, that You have created us to do for Your good pleasure, and in doing all that You have called us to do. We will have unspeakable joy knowing that we are in line with Your will for our lives.

We are Your servants Lord and we will go in the way in

which You want us to go. We ask that You continue to equip us, continue to draw near to us as we draw near to You, and continue to love us in spite of ourselves. Lord in the midst of it all we will praise You.

We will praise You on the mountain and in the valley because we know that You are with us, we can do anything with You and we will do everything for You. We couldn't or wouldn't do it for anyone else but we will do it for You.

We will climb the mountain, stay in the valley, soar through the storm, kill the giant and stand in the rain for YOU. We will do it for You because we know that we can do all things through You and for You because You strengthen us.

We present our body and all that we are. We are Your living sacrifice. It is our choice to be good, acceptable and perfect in Your glorious will. After all that You have done for us this is the least we can do for You. We rejoice with gladness in being a vessel. We give You the authority to use us. In Jesus' name! To God to be GLORY!!!!!

Reflections:

The Fight

$\mathcal{G}$od is not a man that He should lie, but He is the truth and the light. He is my ever-present help. I praise Him today for being all that I need and every thing that I want. I sit as a hungry servant worshipping and giving Him praise. Thanking Him for His presence, because without His presence I will not be, if He does not direct me I will not go, If He does not speak through me I will not speak, it is truly all about Him for He is my direction, my revelation and my protection. It's Him alone: that I seek to be near, that I draw to, that I glorify and magnify, that meets my every need, that I receive unconditional love from, that I worship, that I can't live without. **(Ps. 48:1) "Great is the LORD, and greatly to be praised in the city of our God, in the mountain of his holiness. "**

Sometimes because of life on life terms we have to fight, but if we fight with our own strength we will get weak and tired. God speaks to us and says, "let me fight for you." It is then that our fight becomes a different fight. When we feel a fight coming on it is essential that we draw to God to strengthen up. After the fight we understand that we are always going to be VICTORIOUS because we are mighty through HIM.

We have to be clear on where our help, strength, love, peace and healing comes from, that late in the midnight hour we know who to call on, that we allow God to be everything we need and all that we want, that in the moment of preparation for the fight we call on the God who promises us unfailing love, that our God, the God we love and the God that loves us can do anything and will do everything we ask of Him in line with His will. **(Ps. 88: 1-4) "O LORD God of my salvation, I have cried day and night before thee: Let my prayer come before thee: incline thine ear unto my cry; For my soul is full of troubles: and my life draweth nigh unto the grave. I am counted with them that go down into the pit: I am as a man that hath no strength"**

I pray that we would allow Him to be our strength when we are weak. **(Ps. 84:1-4) "How amiable are thy tabernacles, O LORD of hosts! My soul longeth, yea, even fainteth for the courts of the LORD: my heart and my flesh crieth out for the living God. Yea, the sparrow hath found an house, and the swallow a nest for herself, where she may lay her young, even thine altars, O LORD of hosts, my King, and my God. Blessed are they that dwell in thy house: they will be still praising thee."**

I pray that in the midst of all circumstances we dwell with Him and praise Him for giving us a dwelling place. VICTORY is OURS! To God be the GLORY!

Additional References: Hebrews 4:15-16, Exodus 14:14, Joshua 23:10

Reflections:

His Mirror

*T*have a thankful heart. I thank God for all that He continues to show me. I thank Him for the anointing that He has favored me to have for such a time as this. This time has proved to be a time of growth, preparation to do mighty things in His name, and giving Him the Glory in all ways.

I thank Him for the process to maturity in the spirit, and a vision of who HE created me to be for His purpose. I'm thankful that I have a grateful heart and full heart. **(Ps.103:1-2) "Bless the LORD, O my soul: and all that is within me, bless his holy name. Bless the LORD, O my soul, and forget not all his benefits:"**

I pray that we fully know who God is. We cannot fully know who we are until we recognize who God is. He is the author and the finisher. He is the lover of our soul, the healer of our past, the mind regulator, the foundation of our present and the goal setter of our future.

I pray that: when we look at ourselves in the mirror, we ask God what He sees and walk in what He tells us, that we would use the Bible as a tool to find ourselves, that we read the words that say we are fearfully and wonderfully made, that we are the head and not the tail, that we have been created in the image of God, Himself, that we would get a God understanding of whom we are, that when we feel misunderstood by people, we would be healed by the understanding of who God says we are.

I pray: that we would not be plagued by our past, that we will not live through our mistakes, but that we would live through our Father's words about us, that we would continue to envision our Father standing with open arms ready to receive us, a Father that is there even when we turn from Him, a Father that will never give up on us, a Father who has given us an identity, a Father who desires to have an intimate relationship with us, who sees our heart, hears our cry and answers our prayers, a Father who loves us in spite of ourselves. Look through His mirror and see yourself. **(1John 4: 16-17) "And so we know and RELY on the love God has for us. GOD is LOVE. Whoever lives in love lives in God, and God in him. In this way, love is made complete among us so that we will have confidence on the Day of Judgment, because in this world we are like him. We love because he first loved us."** To God be the Glory!

Additional References: Ps.31:15, 46:10, Isaiah 61:3, John 6:37, book suggestion: Beauty for Ashes by Joyce Myer

Reflections:

Love Worth Finding

$\mathcal{I}$ praise a worthy God. MY GOD. I thank God for wholeness, completeness and abundance of happiness. God alone is able and worthy of my complete trust. I thank God that as I abide in Him, He will abide in me. **(Ps. 48:1) "Great is the Lord, and most worthy of praise."**

I pray that we realize that loving someone in the flesh is costly. It can cost us to go emotionally bankrupt if we don't know whom our source is or if loving that person is out of God's will for our lives.

I pray that when our heart has been shattered into pieces that we would collect the pieces and take them to the lover of our soul. It is these pieces that can cause the hurt to be so strong that we can physically feel our chest caving in, it is that time that the Holy Spirit can show us the source of our pain or it is then that we draw to our daddy-God. It is then that we can open ourselves up for the healing power of our Father.

I pray that: we see the source, we ask the Holy Spirit to show us the things that we are mature enough to see and then cast them over to our heart fixer. Our soul will weep over our emptiness, but as we cry the tears of a broken heart, we have an open door to God to take those tears and refresh us with every single one of them.

I pray: that God will restore our soul, regulate our mind, direct our gaze and lead us to the center of where true love abides - in Him, when another person does not love us as we would have hoped, or when we would have hoped, that we find ourselves in GOD, that we never stray too far away from the God that has promised us unconditional love, the God who always has His arms open to receive us when we get hurt.

I pray that God will heal us of all our pain and that we would join with Him so that He will make us whole again. I ask God to forgive us if we have ever given someone else His place. I thank God that His love always finds us and meets us where we are to bring us back to where we need to be. I love God with all my heart and with all my soul and because of that I pray that we shall not stray to look for fleshly love that will always disappoint us if we try to raise it to the standard of God. I pray that God will always have the biggest and best place in our lives and that no matter what emptiness, will not over take us. Love is great, love from one to another is what God created us to enjoy and appreciate but His love HAS TO COME FIRST, His love has to be the foundation. It is only God who promises to love us in spite of ourselves. We can love people unconditionally, we cannot expect them to be perfect, but we can ask God to per fect them as well as us in Him. To God Be the GLORY!

Additional   References: 2Corinthians   5:14,13:11, Ephesians 3;19, 1John 4:7, John 14:14, Chronicles 7:14

Reflections:

He is Great

~

*G*od is Good. He is worthy of our honor, and of our praises. I am thankful that He has called me His own. I am thankful that I am all He created me to be. He made me in His image and I give Him thanks and praises.

He is the lifter of my head and my joy late in the midnight hour. He gives me joy in the midst of the process and for that I am thankful. I am thankful that He loves me in spite of myself. I worship Him for who He is and who He is preparing me to be for Him. **(Hebrews 12:28-29) "Wherefore we receiving a kingdom which cannot be moved, let us have grace, whereby we may serve God acceptably with reverence and godly fear: For our God is a consuming fire."**

I pray: that we would, as Christians, walk in a love that shows in our words, actions, and smile, that more and more people would see the grace on our lives that God has given us. We must RE PRE SENT God in all that we say and do. He is awesome and worthy of all the praises.

I pray that we would see Him as our ultimate comforter, our sole provider, our beginning and our end, our peace and strength, our heart fixer, and our best friend. He is all that we need and more than able to give us all that we want. All we have to do is seek Him first, line up with His will for our lives and submit to Him as servants. We have the opportunity to ask God for many things. He will give us what we want even if it's not what He wants for us, but the only things that we can ask for is what we see. Imagine for one moment allowing Him to give us what He wants us to have. The Bible says that He will give us exceedingly and abundantly above all that we shall ever ask for or think of.

So, my prayer for us today is that we would give up the things that we want, seek Him and allow Him to give us what He wants us to have. God gave us a will so we can have what we will, but it won't ever compare to His will for our lives. Decide today: to live God's purpose or seek God's face to find out what your purpose is or live a saved life that's just o.k. God is perfecting our life, after fixing the mess that we made of it, trying to get to where we thought we wanted and needed to be, it is in the fixing that God gets all the Glory.

Negative situations can always turn into positive if we allow God to control them. People can speak negativity into our life, but it's up to us to respond with positive FAITH. People who always have an opinion base it on their experience. People who have faith base their opinion on GOD. I pray that we become and remain Positive thinkers, speakers, and examples that Jesus was to us, that we become and remain more and more like Him daily. To God be the Glory!

Additional References: Isaiah 9:6, Nahum 1:7, Ps.32:7-11, Romans 8:28, Mark 11:2

Reflections:

Who Do You Need Him to Be?

⁓

I pray that we will find all that we need in the God we glorify. Praise His wonderful name, which is above all names. I worship Him for who He is, and who He has been, and who He promises He will always be to me. I'm thankful that when I ask Him to give me peace in my mind, comfort in my heart and rest for my body, that He gives them to me that I might be refreshed, full of compassion and joy for the one who gave me all things. I have a thankful heart and a grateful spirit. **(Ps. 34:1-4) "I will extol the Lord at all times; his praise will always be on my lips. My soul boasts in the Lord; let the afflicted hear and rejoice. Glorify the Lord with me; let us exalt his name together. I sought the Lord and he answered me and delivered me from all my fears."**

GOD IS GOOD! When we need an instructor, counselor and a teacher. **(Ps. 32: 8) "I will instruct you and teach you in the way you should go; I will counsel you and watch over you."** When we need unfailing love. **(Ps. 32: 10) "Many are the woes of the wicked, but the Lord's unfailing love surrounds the man who TRUSTS in him." (Emphasis mine).**

I pray that we would call on Him before we call on anyone else when we are in need, that we would recognize whom He is to us and that He can meet our every need. When we need a restorer **(Ps. 23:3) "He restores my soul. When we need a light in the midst of what seems like darkness" (John 12:12) "When Jesus spoke again to the people, he said, "I am the light of the world. Whoever follows me will never walk in darkness, but will have the light of life."**

When we need a healer and affirmation for the power He has given us **(Malachi 4: 2-3) "But for you who revere my name, the sun of righteousness will rise with healing in its wings. And you will go out and leap like calves released from the stall. Then you will TRAMPLE down the wicked; they will be ashes under the soles of your feet on the day when I do these things, says the Lord Almighty."** (Emphasis mine)

When we need a hiding place and protection **(Ps. 32:7) "You are my hiding place; you will protect me from promises to give us the desires of our heart."**

Everything we need we can find in Him, but we must hold Him to His word and everything that He has promised us, remind Him **(Ps. 16) "I will praise the Lord who counsels me; even at NIGHT my HEART instructs me. I have set the Lord always before me. Because he is at my right hand I will not be SHAKEN. Therefore my heart is glad and my tongue rejoices; my body also will REST SECURE, because you will not ABANDON me to the grave, nor will you let your holy one see decay. You have made known to me the path of life; you will fill me with JOY in your presence, with eternal pleasures at your right hand."** To God be the GLORY!!!!

Additional References: Colossians 2:6-7, Malachi 4:2-3, Isaiah 25:4, Ps.23, John 15:7

Reflections:

God, I Choose:

To habitually be Christ like
To practice Christ like character
To accept every assignment
To be used to make a difference
in the lives of people around me
To be available to serve and be a servant
To rejoice in You always
To not be ruled by temptation
To commit my mind and body to You
To gradually grow more and more like Christ daily
To humbly look at the truth about me
To allow You to make the necessary changes in me
To surrender my failures, faults, pride,
mistakes and or sin to You
To allow You to teach me in all my ways
To have a teachable attitude that I might grow in You
To rely on Your word for direction
To love You even when You feel distant
To give You all of my heart, mind and strength
To worship You in spite of how I feel
To make Your word the first and final authority in my life
To not focus on the pain, but on the plan
To allow the pain to build Jesus – like character in me
To rest in Christ in the midst of distress
To focus on the promises of God
and not on my present circumstances
To surrender to Your transformation
To praise You even when I feel
You have removed Yourself from me
To let go of my old ways
To put on daily the character of Christ
To make a commitment to You that I might walk through
life doing what You have purposed for me to do

To know You and love You
To intentionally change my thoughts and my ways to
Christ-like thoughts and ways
To fill my life with the word
To trust You even when I don't understand You
To allow You to reproduce Your character in me
To be obedient to You that I may unlock
Your power in my life
To have a relationship with Jesus,
a relationship that is personal, but not private

GOD, My greatest desire is to please You, to be a witness of Your goodness, and to love as You love. I choose to make being like You a habit.

Love, Love and Love

I'm thankful, grateful and overjoyed because I am loved. The ultimate lover, the lover that loved me when I was unlovable, loves me. GLORY, GLORY, GLORY. Thank You Jesus, thank You, for giving Your life so that I may have eternal life. Thank You for standing up for me when no one else would. Thank You for giving me purpose, a purpose that is filled with Your guidance. **(Ps.31:14-15a) "But I trusted in thee, O Jehovah: I said, Thou art my God. My times are in thy hand"**

I pray that we love others as we love Jesus, that we carry our cross. The cross that is made vertical and horizontal. Our vertical is our relationship with God and our horizontal is our relationship with people. We cannot have intimate worship with God and be unable to love people. If we are laid on the cross we are not stretched vertically, but we are stretched horizontally. It is easier to love the lover of our soul, the God who has made us whole. It is not as easy to love the people around us who hurt us, disappoint us, judge us, betray us and/or are disloyal to us.

I pray that God would equip us, that He would prepare us, that He would deposit in us the love that He wants us not only to show others, but also to give others, that we look at people through His eyes, that we see them as He sees them, that God would give us the strength to deal with people as He has dealt with us.

God requires us to love our sisters and brothers not because they deserve it but because He deserves it. He deserves our best even when we've been hurt. He deserves our obedience even when it requires us to do something that does not feel good. **(1John 3: 23) "And this is his commandment, that we should believe on the name of his Son Jesus Christ, and love one another, as he gave us commandment." (Luke 6:31-36) "And as ye would that men should do to you, do ye also to them likewise. For if ye love them which love you, what thank have ye? For sinners also love those that love them. And if ye do good to them which do good to you, what thank have ye? For sinners also do even the same. And if ye lend to them of whom ye hope to receive, what thank have ye? For sinners also lend to sinners, to receive as much again. But love ye your enemies, and do good, and lend, hoping for nothing again; and your reward shall be great, and ye shall be the children of the Highest: for he is kind unto the unthankful and to the evil. Be ye therefore merciful, as your Father also is merciful."** To God be the Glory!

Additional References: 1John 4:7, 4:12, Leviticus 19:18, Mark 12:31

Reflections:

Let Us Pray

Pray with me knowing that we are asking for change, change that may not always feel good to our flesh.

*D*ear Heavenly Father,

We come to You in the name that is above all names, we come to You thanking You for the sacrifice of Your son Jesus, we come to You asking You to help us have forgiving, loving, gentle, pure hearts.

We want hearts that do what they were created to do. Hearts just like Yours. Hearts that love people based on You. Hearts that don't see, but feel compassion for the people You have put around us to get a greater look at who You are. We want hearts that are on fire and filled with passion. Search our hearts Lord and remove anything that is not like you. We ask that you put the shattered pieces of our heart back together, restore us. Give us a right spirit that we might daily be more and more like You.

Lord, we ask that You be Lord over every area of our lives and teach us to release, re pre sent, reveal You to the lives of people who don't know You as we do. We want to have everything that is like You that we might talk like You, walk like You and think like You.

We desire to be right, we desire to be whole and we desire to live life as You have predestined us to live it. We thank You that You died for us, we thank You that You live in us. **(John 3: 16) "For God so loved the world, that he gave his only begotten Son, that whosoever believeth in him should not perish, but have everlasting life."**

Lord, we pray that daily You will give us the strength that we need to get to You, to draw to You, draw from You, draw near to You and draw people to You. In the mighty name of Jesus Amen! To God be the Glory!

<u>Reflections:</u>

If I Could Just Touch

〜

God is so good; He's so good to me. I thank Him for freedom, security, worth- beyond measure, beauty, wisdom and a sense of belonging to someone – HIM. I worship Him and in the midst of that worship I give and receive a love that is above all love.

In the midst of my worship I can feel the power of affection, intimacy, appreciation being shared between Him and I. What a mighty God I worship, love and praise because it is Him who is worthy of my all. **(Ps. 56:3-4) "What time I am afraid, I will trust in thee. In God I will praise his word, in God I have put my trust; I will not fear what flesh can do unto me."**

One of my favorite passages:

(Mark 5:25-29) "And a certain woman, which had an issue of blood twelve years, And had suffered many things of many physicians, and had spent all that she had, and was nothing bettered, but rather grew worse, When she had heard of Jesus, came in the press behind, and touched his garment. For she said, if I may touch but his clothes, I shall be whole. Immediately her bleeding stopped and she felt in her body that she was freed from her suffering."

I pray that we know where to go in the midst of our suffering, that we know how to speak of Jesus in such a way that a person who doesn't know Jesus as we do, and is suffering, will feel drawn to Him through us to be healed, that we confidently know there is a God that can do immediately what many times we expect people to do. We can give people years of opportunity and yet our needs are still not met, people can disappoint us and give us more pain than we had before we went to them.

I pray that we have a relationship with the ultimate healer so we know where to go **first** and don't put pressure on people to do for us **ONLY** what God can do, that no matter what we are going through if we can just drag our afflicted body to His presence and receive just a touch, because it is in His presence that there is healing for our pain, there is fullness of joy, unconditional love, comfort, everything we need is in His presence.

I pray that when we are going through something we don't go though it for twelve years or twelve days depending on someone or something for our healing, but that we get right into the presence of the God who loved us before we even loved ourselves. Get in His presence because in His presence we can find all that we need. To God be the Glory!

Additional References: Ps.84:11, Ps.55:17, Isaiah 65:24, 2Chronicles 15:2, Deuteronomy 31:8

Reflections:

Fill My Cup Lord

〜

*P*raise the God who is worthy of all praises let the fruit of my lips and the power of my tongue praise the highest God. He has deemed me worthy to do His will. **(1Chronicles 16:29) "worship the Lord in the beauty of holiness"**

When we suffer we draw to God and we lose more and more of our self. Suffering occurs when we are being emptied out but suffering becomes tolerable when we run to the arms of God. His arms are always open and when He takes us in His arms, He replenishes us with Him because we are becoming empty of us. So, if we know where to go when things become uncomfortable, suffering doesn't last long. I was talking to some sisters last night and one of them said, " when does suffering end" I said, "when we stop looking at it as suffering." Take a dirty glass, we don't want to drink anything out of a dirty glass. A glass has to be completely empty and washed clean before fresh living water can be poured in it. When the suffering occurs God wants to empty and wash us COMPLETELY of any dirt. He wants to wash us clean and then pour fresh living water in us. God wants us to be like that dirty glass. He wants us to be completely emptied and perfected in Him.

I challenge you today to take a glass that is clearly dirty and pour water into it. Sit it on your kitchen sink and every morning pour a little water out. As you pour it out ask God to show you, as you are pouring it out, what He is removing or perfecting in you. At this time we want to confirm to God that we want Him, we are open to changing and we are open to being emptied. Don't pour any more water out until you recognize and change whatever it is He has shown you. God does not expect us to get patience in one day, but He does expect us daily to grow towards being more patient. Then we can pour a little more water out and when our glass is completely empty wash it clean and praise Him as you are doing it. Ask God to purify your mind, purge your spirit, cleanse your heart, peel off the residue, put the broken pieces back together, detoxify your body and help you to not be moved by emotion or circumstance. Now fill your glass with fresh water a little at a time until your glass is full and every time you put a little water in it ask God to fill your cup, make yourself available to Him until your cup is overflowing and as that cup sits there full everyday and circumstances happen that you don't understand thank God that you trust Him enough to praise Him in spite of because you are full of peace, love, His spirit and fresh living water. To God be the Glory!

Additional References: Jeremiah 31:1-4, 13-14, Isaiah 60:5,15-17,19-20, John 15:5

Reflections:

God Said It

*P*raise the Lord. He is worthy! I'm thankful for His love because He loved me even before I loved myself. His love is not based on my accomplishments but His love is based on who He is. **(Ps.100: 1-2) "Make a joyful noise unto the LORD, all ye lands. Serve the LORD with gladness: come before his presence with singing."**

I pray that we would confidently be knowledgeable about what God said in His word. **(Deuteronomy 28: 12-13) "The LORD shall open unto thee his good treasure, the heaven to give the rain unto thy land in his season, and to bless all the work of thine hand: and thou shalt lend unto many nations, and thou shalt not borrow. And the LORD shall make thee the head, and not the tail; and thou shalt be above only, and thou shalt not be beneath; if that thou hearken unto the commandments of the LORD thy God, which I command thee this day, to observe and to do them."**

I pray that we are in line with His commandments so that our visions are not made up or created by this world, but based and created on the reality of God and His promises. **(Isaiah 43: 1-2) "But now thus saith the LORD that created thee, O Jacob, and he that formed thee, O Israel, Fear not: for I have redeemed thee, I have called thee by thy name; thou art mine. When thou passest through the waters, I will be with thee; and through the**

rivers, they shall not overflow thee: when thou walkest through the fire, thou shalt not be burned; neither shall the flame kindle upon thee."

God has called us by name and claimed us. We have nothing to fear. So, if we have to pass through some issues, let's go right through them. We may even go through and come out with a couple of scars, but none that God can't heal. Those scars were allowed by God to make us stronger. We must confront and walk through those problems, through those fires having all confidence in knowing that God is with us. He is always there for us, it may be to heal us, it may be to protect us, and it may even be to walk with us to ensure us that we can't stop, He's there.

Walk your walk, walk it, even when it hurts and know that God will not allow any pain to destroy us. He will only allow us to see the extent of the fire and when we come out of it, we will look back and say, "I made it." We have made it through some things that should of made us lose our mind, we have been through some things that should have killed us, we have been through some things that should have destroyed us, but " WE ARE STILL HERE" because God has a plan for our lives and He is going to use us for something greater than we can ever imagine. He is going to use us that He might "GET ALL THE GLORY ." TO GOD BE THE GLORY!

Additional References: Ps.145:18, John 7:37,14:21

Reflections:

Praise Him

≈

*H*e is great! Worship the Lord your God in your own way. Let Him know it is this day that you proclaim your love for Him.

(Ps. 95: 1-3) "Come let us sing for joy; let us shout aloud to the Rock of our salvation. Let us come before him with thanksgiving and extol him with music and song. For the Lord is the great God, the great King above all gods."

(Ps. 96: 1-4) " O sing unto the LORD a new song: sing unto the LORD, all the earth. Sing unto the LORD, bless his name; shew forth his salvation from day to day. Declare his glory among the heathen, his wonders among all people. For the LORD is great, and greatly to be praised."

(Ps. 33: 1) "Rejoice in the LORD, O ye righteous: for praise is comely for the upright."

(2Chronicles 5: 13) "It came even to pass, as the trumpeters and singers were as one, to make one sound to be heard in praising and thanking the LORD; and when they lifted up their voice with the trumpets and cymbals and instruments of music, and praised the LORD, saying, For he is good; for his mercy endureth for ever: that then the house was filled with a cloud, even the house of the LORD."

(Ps. 100:1-5) " Make a joyful noise unto the LORD, all ye lands. Serve the LORD with gladness: come before his presence with singing. Know ye that the LORD he is

God: it is he that hath made us, and not we ourselves; we are his people, and the sheep of his pasture. Enter into his gates with thanksgiving, and into his courts with praise: be thankful unto him, and bless his name. For the LORD is good; his mercy is everlasting; and his truth endureth to all generations."

(Revelation 4:8&11) "Day and night they never stop saying "Holy, Holy, Holy is the Lord God Almighty, who was, and is, and is to come. You are worthy, our Lord and God, to receive glory and honor and power, for you created all things, and by your will they were created and have their being." HE IS WORTHY! PRAISE HIM ANY HOW! PRAISE HIM IN SPITE OF! (Romans 12: 12) "Be joyful in hope, patient in affliction, and faithful in prayer." To God be the Glory

<u>Additional References</u>: Ephesians 5:19, Proverbs 27:2, Ps.42:5,11,43:5

<u>Reflections:</u>

Humility

God is a Good God, a Merciful God, a Marvelous God, a Wonderful God, a Gentle God and much, much, more God and for that I am forever thankful, grateful and indebted to my Father who has promised me many things and who has given me much more already than I am deserving of. **(Ps.103: 1-5) "Bless the LORD, O my soul: and all that is within me, bless his holy name. Bless the LORD, O my soul, and forget not all his benefits: Who forgiveth all thine iniquities; who healeth all thy diseases; Who redeemeth thy life from destruction; who crowneth thee with lovingkindness and tender mercies; Who satisfieth thy mouth with good things; so that thy youth is renewed like the eagle's."**

I pray that we become humble imitators in the sight of the Lord **(Philippians 2: 3-8) "Let nothing be done through strife or vainglory; but in lowliness of mind let each esteem other better than themselves. Look not every man on his own things, but every man also on the things of others. Let this mind be in you, which was also in Christ Jesus: Who, being in the form of God, thought it not robbery to be equal with God: But made himself of no reputation, and took upon him the form of a servant, and was made in the likeness of men: And being found in fashion as a man, he humbled himself, and became obedient unto death, even the death of the cross."**

I pray that we all get our strength from God to carry our cross in humility, that we realize that we have been put here, in this position, to endure this circumstance, to handle this problem, to handle this success, to handle this rejection, to handle this dispute, to do whatever God has already predestined and knew that we would have to go through. We are here to do His will. (**Micah 6:8**) **"He hath shewed thee, O man, what is good; and what doth the LORD require of thee, but to do justly, and to love mercy, and to walk humbly with thy God?"**

It is not about us. It is all about Him. It is about the walk that He requires us to walk. We cannot get so caught up in our needs or pleasing someone else's needs before we please the FATHER. If we are lined up in His will He will supply all of our needs. Please Him and we will be pleased. If we submit to His desires, those desires will become our desires. The desires for exceedingly abundantly and God will give us those desires. Bless God through prayer, praise and thanksgiving and He will bless you. To God be the Glory!

Additional References: Proverbs 15:33, 2Chronicles 33:12, Proverbs 16:19, 1Peter 5:6-7

Reflections:

Dwell With Us

*P*s.139 says that I am **"fearfully and wonderfully made."** I will walk in that, I will walk in who He says I am and in the meantime, in the in between time I will bless Him and praise Him all the way to the gates of heaven. **(Ps.99:5) "worship at his footstool! he is holy."**

I pray that we would rest in the midst of all that we go through knowing that our God has created us and made us in His image. We do not fight any battles on our own but let Him fight them for us. God knows our beginning and our end. He knows what we go through, when we go through.

I pray that we rest in these words. **(Genesis. 50:20) "But as for you, ye thought evil against me; but God meant it unto good, to bring to pass, as it is this day, to save much people alive." (Ps.21:11) "For they intended evil against thee: they imagined a mischievous device, which they are not able to perform."** Character is being built in us. We are daily becoming more and more like Him. That is why it is imperative to stay close to Him that we might know the direction to take – His direction.

(Ps. 91:1-2) "He that dwelleth in the secret place of the most High shall abide under the shadow of the Almighty. I will say of the LORD, He is my refuge and my fortress: my God; in him will I trust." (Ps. 91:14) "Because he hath set his love upon me, therefore will I deliver him: I will set him on high, because he hath known

my name." Because we love Him, He will take care of us.

I pray that we press towards the prize that we know that our God has a plan for our lives and we must not give up. **(Philippians 3: 13-14) "Brethren, I count not myself to have apprehended: but this one thing I do, forgetting those things which are behind, and reaching forth unto those things which are before, I press toward the mark for the prize of the high calling of God in Christ Jesus."**

I pray that we would remain focused on the will of God, that we will seek the Kingdom of God, that the Holy Spirit would daily Reign in us, give us a fresh anointing, that in our weakness God gives us strength.

(2Corinthians12: 9-10) "And he said unto me, My grace is sufficient for thee: for my strength is made perfect in weakness. Most gladly therefore will I rather glory in my infirmities, that the power of Christ may rest upon me. Therefore I take pleasure in infirmities, in reproaches, in necessities, in persecutions, in distresses for Christ's sake: for when I am weak, then am I strong." (Romans 12: 12) "Rejoicing in hope; patient in tribulation; continuing instant in prayer;" To God be the Glory!

<u>**Additional References**</u>: Ps.32,144:1-2, Proverbs 18:10

<u>**Reflections:**</u>

Prayer

Prepare your hearts for prayer, clear your minds for purity, and rest in this moment knowing that the next one will be a moment of expectancy for greatness to evolve.

Lord, we ask that if there is anything that is not of You in our lives for You to remove it. Help us to draw on You for our needs. Help us to look at You as our source and guide. **(2Timothy 2: 26) "That they may come to their senses and escape the snare of the devil, having been taken captive by him to do his will."**

Lord, we want to obey You in every way. Break the spirit of fear, pride, doubt, and unforgiveness that may be keeping us from walking in obedience. We have acknowledged You as our Savior. We ask that You guide us to relationships that will edify and glorify You.

No matter what happens, we are certain that we are not without hope. We have faith, but Lord, we ask that You strengthen that faith right in this moment. We ask that You give us a heart of You. We ask that we not just read these prayers but we allow them to get in our spirit. God with every request that has been made, we ask that we not get confused when the request is not granted.

We know that You are not the author of confusion and we will walk in perfect peace and we ask in all things You give us understanding. We will walk and not faint, and we will draw to You and know with all confidence that our steps are ordered by You and ALL THINGS WORK TOGETHER FOR THE GOOD because we love You, magnify You, worship You and praise You in spite of. We trust You. Lord, rest in our heart, fill our mind, wrap Your arms around us and love us in spite of our self. To GOD be the GLORY!!!

<u>Reflections:</u>

He Predestined and Foreknew Us

$\mathcal{I}$ will bless the Lord at all times. I adore the highest God. I am thankful this day that I have an intimate lover. A lover who loves above and beyond any love that I have ever imagined. He's so good to me. I raise my hands and lift my head and as I raise my hands I wave them in the air to confuse the devil.

The devil said I should be depressed, sad and lonely, and the moment he thinks I'm listening to him, I put my hands in the air and say God I worship and praise You. I thank Him that I'm never lonely, alone, but not lonely because everything I need is in His presence. **(Acts 24:14) " worship I the God of my fathers"**

I pray that we don't allow the devil to have his way, that we glorify our God who has predestined us, that we know He has a plan for our lives and He has given us everything we need to fulfill that plan. **(Romans 8: 29-32) "For whom he did foreknow, he also did predestinate to be conformed to the image of his Son, that he might be the first-born among many brethren. Moreover whom he did predestinate, them he also called: and whom he called, them he also justified: and whom he justified, them he also glorified. What shall we then say to these things? If God be for us, who can be against us? He that spared not**

his own Son, but delivered him up for us all, how shall he not with him also freely give us all things?" God has given us power, strength, endurance and His Son.

I pray: that we trust, believe and have faith during all the circumstances of life that we utilize the tools that God has given us, that we conform to His ways and let His will be done in our lives even when His promises look impossible. Impossibilities move us and all others out of God's way, and all we can do is watch Him work. God wants to use us to let Him be the center of attention so we have to move our issues, our pride, our agenda, our confusion, our fear and our will out of the way and be conformed, so that God can let His will be done and do exceedingly, abundantly above all that we could ever ask or think of.

(Romans 8: 24-25) "For we are saved by hope: but hope that is seen is not hope: for what a man seeth, why doth he yet hope for? But if we hope for that we see not, then do we with patience wait for it." To God be the Glory!

<u>**Additional References**</u>: Ps.145:18; Colossians2:6-7, Isaiah26:4, Ephesians 2:10, 6:13

<u>**Reflections:**</u>

I Trust Him

$\sim\!\!\!\sim$

 love Him, I trust Him, and I magnify my God's name above all other names. There is no confusion as to who I'm speaking about, He is the lover of my soul, the lifter of my head, my ever present help, my strength when I am weak, my light when it is dark, my healer when I am hurting, my lover when I am lonely and my armor when I am at war. My God! **(Ps.18:1-3) "I will love thee, O Lord, my strength. The LORD is my rock, and my fortress, and my deliverer; my God, my strength, in whom I will trust; my buckler, and the horn of my salvation, and my high tower. I will call upon the LORD, who is worthy to be praised."** I pray: that no matter what our eyes see that we would not allow them to determine our circumstances, that things that look impossible to us are the things that God works with, because NOTHING IS IMPOSSIBLE WITH HIM, that we listen to God's word over our lives, that we rejuvenate, revive, recommit, refuel, remember and remain in our intimate relationship with God, that our relationship with Him is never affected by our circumstances, that we trust Him in all things and lean not to our own understanding, that we continue to adore Him even in the hard times because it is the hard test that continue to build our spiritual maturity, it is the hard test that gives us greater victory and it is during the hard test that we should draw near to the one who promises to **(Hebrews 13:5b) "for he hath said, I will** never leave thee, nor forsake thee." (John 14: 1) "Let not your heart be troubled: ye believe in God, believe also in me." (John 16: 20-23) "Verily, verily, I say unto you, that ye shall weep and lament, but the world shall rejoice: and ye shall be sorrowful, but your sorrow shall be turned into joy. A woman when she is in travail hath sorrow, because her hour is come: but as soon as she is delivered of the child, she remembereth no more the anguish, for joy that a man is born into the world. And ye now therefore have sorrow: but I will see you again, and your heart shall rejoice, and your joy no man taketh from you. <u>And in that day ye shall ask me nothing. Verily, verily, I say unto you, whatsoever ye shall ask the Father in my name, he will give it you.</u>" (emphasis mine)

I pray for our endured strength, our renewed trust and our constant love for our Father whose plans are for our Good. The Lord said: **(Joel 2:25) "And I will restore to you the years that the locust hath eaten, the cankerworm, and the caterpiller, and the palmerworm, my great army which I sent among you."** To God be the Glory!

<u>Additional References</u>: Job 13:15, Ps.25:2,31:6, Isaiah 50:10

<u>Reflections:</u>

His Words, and His Ways

〰

*P*raise Him! Worship Him! What a mighty God! He is worthy of my all. I lift my hands and praise Him for He is good and His mercy endures forever. **(Ps. 47: 1-2) "O clap your hands, all ye people; shout unto God with the voice of triumph."**

I will sing praise with my mouth, worship with my hands, love Him with my heart, listen with my spiritual ear and see His goodness with my faithful eye. I love Him for where He brought me from, for the places He's taking me to, for the circumstances that He keeps bringing me through, for the unlimited comfort He gives to me and for the love He has shown me in all things I give Him praise. **(Hebrews 12: 28) "Wherefore we receiving a kingdom which cannot be moved, let us have grace, whereby we may serve God acceptably with reverence and godly fear."**

I pray: that we are all in God's perfect will, that we daily seek His face, and seek His will for our lives, that we walk in the spirit, not in the flesh, that we seek to do all that we can do for the Kingdom of God, that no confusion lie in our mind, no pain lie in our body, and no disappointment lie in our heart, that He gives us peace in the midst of all situations, that He heals the pain of today that we might face tomorrow, that we stand on God's word, that we rely on His promises, that we hold close to His presence, that nothing will overwhelm us, but that we would cast all of our cares over to

Him, that we not only know Gods acts, but that we know His ways, that we allow God to sustain us with His ways, that once we know God's way we will give up our way.

(Proverbs 8:32) "Now therefore hearken unto me, O ye children: for blessed are they that keep my ways." (Isaiah 55:8) "For my thoughts are not your thoughts, neither are your ways my ways, saith the LORD." (Isaiah 58:2) "Yet they seek me daily, and delight to know my ways" (1Kings 11:38) "And it shall be, if thou wilt hearken unto all that I command thee, and wilt walk in my ways, and do that is right in my sight, to keep my statutes and my commandments, as David my servant did; that I will be with thee, and build thee a sure house, as I built for David."

I pray: that God finds a home in the obedient hearts of us, His people, that we would want Him to live comfortably inside of us, so daily we seek Him for direction in spite of our circumstances we continue to move in His way and in His will. To God be the Glory!

Additional References: Colossians 2:6-7, John 14:21, Luke 11:28

Reflections:

He's All I Need

*P*raise Him! Praise Him in all that we say and do. I praise God for He is worthy! I adore Him. He is everything that I need and all that I want. He is the strength I need to walk, the knowledge I need to talk and the direction I need to go in. He is so great and so faithful. I must do my part, the part that He has given me to do, to give love to the unlovely, to love unconditionally and to love based on Him and not based on what people have done for me, to me, or with me.

I thank Him for loving me in the pit of hell I was in. I thank Him for saving me and loving me in spite of myself. I thank Him and I am grateful that He sees what I am and still chooses to use me and lead me to what He wants me to be for Him. **(Revelation 19:10) "And I fell at his feet to worship him."**

I pray: that we get a fire started in our spirit or add some wood to the one we have, that we get GOD deep down in our soul so that when we need Him all we have to do is ask Him to rise up in us, that we stand on our solid foundation, our unshakeable, unmovable, unfearful foundation. We must be forever faithful in our prayer life, we must pray without ceasing, in all that we say and do, we must pray. **(Ps. 63: 1-8) "O God, thou art my God; early will I seek thee: my soul thirsteth for thee, my flesh longeth for thee in a dry and thirsty land, where no water is; to see thy power and** thy glory, so as I have seen thee in the sanctuary. **Because thy loving-kindness is better than life, my lips shall praise thee. Thus will I bless thee while I live: I will lift up my hands in thy name. My soul shall be satisfied as with marrow and fatness; and my mouth shall praise thee with joyful lips: When I remember thee upon my bed, and meditate on thee in the night watches. Because thou hast been my help, therefore in the shadow of thy wings will I rejoice. My soul followeth hard after thee: thy right hand upholdeth me."**

I pray that we would continue in our praise until change comes regardless of where we are we must pray, praise and stay in His presence. **(Exodus 33: 14-15)** **"And he said, My presence shall go with thee, and I will give thee rest. And he said unto him, if thy presence does not go with us do not send us up from here."** To God be the Glory!

<u>Additional References</u>: Hebrews11:6, 1Chronicles28:9, James 4:8, John 16:13, 1Corinthians 2:9-10

<u>Reflections:</u>

Greater is He Who Lives in Me

*G*reat is He. He is wonderful and He is awesome. I call out to my Father and ask Him to love me, to wrap His loving arms around me. I worship Him as I have intimate moments with Him, closing my eyes and dancing with the one who has promised me many things. I love Him because He first loved me. **(Ps. 119:169) "Let my cry come near before thee, O Lord: give me understanding according to thy word."**

I pray that we stand firm on God's promises. It is His promises and our hope that equal faith. God has made promises to us so that in the midst of our circumstances we draw to Him and have faith in what He has already promised us. So, when we feel like we are all alone, we draw to His promises. When we feel like we are ready to give up, we draw to His love and comfort.

(Heb.13: 5b) He promised to **"for he hath said, I will never leave thee, nor forsake thee."** When we feel like everything we have worked for we have lost.

Draw to His promise that **(Joel 2: 25)** He will **"And I will restore to you the years that the locust hath eaten, the cankerworm, and the caterpiller, and the palmerworm."**

When are bills are greater than our paycheck. **(Philippians**

4: 19) Draw to His promise to: **"supply all of our needs according to His riches and in Glory by Christ Jesus."**

When we are confused, depressed, unhappy with our current situation, when things that God has promised look impossible, draw to Him. **(Ps. 16: 11) "Thou wilt shew me the path of life: in thy presence is fulness of joy; at thy right hand there are pleasures for evermore."** (Isaiah **30:21) "And thine ears shall hear a word behind thee, saying, This is the way, walk ye in it, when ye turn to the right hand, and when ye turn to the left."** (Ps. **37: 7a) "Rest in the LORD, and wait patiently for him"** (Romans. **8: 28) "And we know that all things work together for good to them that love God, to them who are the called according to his purpose."**

God has a plan for us. I pray: for renewed strength, greater understanding, detailed directions, joy and peace as we walk the walk that God has predestined us to walk, that we will not give up, that we know the promises of God and recite them in the midst of all situations. Everything we need to sustain us is in the word, seek it and say it, use the word against every action that Satan tries to bring against you. You have access to your sword pick it up and fight!!!! To God be the Glory!!

Additional References: John 7:37, Romans 8:13

Reflections:

Blood Bought Right

❦

*P*raise His worthy and Holy Name. Praise Him! Worship Him! Take a moment and give God all the praise for He is truly worthy. Greater is He that lives in me than He that lives in the world and for that I am grateful and thankful. He is good. **(Ps. 7:17) "I will praise the LORD according to his righteousness: and will sing praise to the name of the LORD most high." (Ps.9:1-2) "I will praise thee, O LORD, with my whole heart; I will shew forth all thy marvelous works. I will be glad and rejoice in thee: I will sing praise to thy name, O thou most High." (Ps. 22:25) "My praise shall be of thee in the great congregation. I will pay my vows before them that fear Him."**

I pray: touching and agreeing in the spirit with all the eyes that read these words that God would move mightily in our favor, that all that is ours be released in Jesus name, that we surrender our will to the will of the Father that He might bless us according to His riches in glory, that we will patiently wait on Him, but if there is anything that is being held we claim it in Jesus' name, we claim the salvation of our families and friends.

I pray: for endurance to run the race, for a clear understanding of what it is that God is doing in our lives, I bind the spirit of depression, sadness, loneliness, confusion, insecurity, fear, condemnation and doubt, that we walk the walk of life with God and not go before Him or lag after Him, that we stay focused and driven not by our emotions, but by the confidence that we have in God to give us all the direction, confidence and vision that we need to live the life of abundant blessings in all phases of our lives, that we submit our will to God's will and that God would prepare us for whatever it is that we have been called to do according to His will, that these things are my blood brought right to have in Jesus' name **(Romans 10: 10-12) "For with the heart man believeth unto righteousness; and with the mouth confession is made unto salvation. For the scripture saith, whosoever believeth on him shall not be ashamed. For there is no difference between the Jew and the Greek: for the same Lord over all is rich unto all that call upon him."** To God be the Glory!

Additional References: Mark 14:24, Luke 22:20, Romans 5:9, Matthew 26:28, Ephesians 1:7

Reflections:

Prayer

〜

Prepare your hearts for prayer, clear your minds for purity, and rest in this moment knowing that the next one will be a moment of expectancy for greatness to evolve.

God, we come to You confidently. We draw near to You and ask that You draw near to us. We humbly seek You, desire to do Your will, and ask for Your help. When we are in pain and our soul needs to be restored.

God, restore our soul. We desperately seek You for Your help and strength. We long to be enveloped in Your arms, to be comforted, safe and at peace. You are so GOOD and You do all things well. Thank You for all of our circumstances, the good and the ones that look bad.

When we are hurting in the midst of that circumstance, we thank You that You are in COMPLETE control, that all things are good for us or You would not permit it.

Thank You for the opportunity to glorify You and magnify Your name. Thank You for what we have learned and what You are continuing to teach us. Use us for Your Glory even if we must suffer through some experiences. Thank You for Your Grace that continues to keep us and give us a renewed sense of Hope. Put our sorrows back down to a manageable level. Help us not to become angry or bitter.

We willingly (**1Peter 4: 13**). **"are partakers of Christ's**

sufferings." We find our comfort and refuge in You while we continue to diligently serve You. We will persevere for Your sake.

(**Matthew 11: 28-30**) "**Come unto me, all ye that labour and are heavy laden, and I will give you rest. Take my yoke upon you, and learn of me; for I am meek and lowly in heart: and ye shall find rest unto your souls. For my yoke is easy, and my burden is light.**" In Jesus' name Amen!

IS THERE ANYTHING TOO HARD FOR GOD? (Genesis 18: 14)

ABSOLUTELY NOT!!!!

To God be the Glory!

Reflections:

He is a Need Meter

I praise the name of the most high and I sit here thankful for the depth of my relationship with Him. Alleluia! I thank Him that the things He has promised me have everything to do with more of Him, His availability to me, and making me more like Him. I'm thankful that I don't need things, I need HIM!

Praise God! Praise Him! Take a moment to praise God who is worthy of all of our praise. I thank God for lifting me up and wrapping His strength around me, whispering in my ear that He loves me. I thank Him that I continuously have a place to go to get joy, comfort, peace and unconditional love. He is great and He is consistent and on this day I thank Him. **(Ps. 40:1) "I waited patiently for the LORD; and he inclined unto me, and heard my cry. "**

I pray: that we call on Him to be the supplier of our every need, that He gives us more of His love, so that He can use us daily to do His will, that He searches our heart and if there is any hardness – he softens it. **(John 16: 20) "Verily, verily, I say unto you, That ye shall weep and lament, but the world shall rejoice: and ye shall be sorrowful, but your sorrow shall be turned into joy."**

I pray: that God will restore our joy, that He will give us joy in the midst of all that we go through daily, that we would keep our joy regardless of the circumstances, regardless of the situations we encounter and regardless of the people we interact with, that God would remind us that He is our joy as long as our focus is Him, that we will be rooted and grounded in Him. **(John 14: 27) "Peace I leave with you, my peace I give unto you: not as the world giveth, give I unto you. Let not your heart be troubled, neither let it be afraid."** I pray that we go to the source, the God who is the supplier of all that we need, the God who promises to meet every need that we have. **(John 15: 7) "If ye abide in me, and my words abide in you, ye shall ask what ye will, and it shall be done unto you."** I pray that we would seek Him FIRST. **(Nahum 1: 7) "The LORD is good, a strong hold in the day of trouble; and he knoweth them that trust in him."** I pray that we trust Him and allow Him to sustain us in all things. I pray for our peace, joy, strength, healing and complete restoration. To God be the Glory!

Additional References: Luke 12:30, Philippians 4:12, Revelation 3:17

Reflections:

I am Empty

∿

*G*lory to the name of the Lord. He is a mighty God. He is worthy to be praised. Daily I will seek more and more of Him. I ask Him to fill me till there is no more of me and only Him.

He has supplied all of my needs even when I didn't recognize Him as the supplier. How thankful I am for the Father who has loved me when I didn't even love myself.

He was the friend that comforted me, when there was no one else. He is my first husband that I have submitted to. He is great and worthy to be praised. I thank Him for being everything I need. **(Judges 5:3) "I, will sing unto the LORD; I will sing praise to the LORD God of Israel."**

I pray: that we will empty ourselves, that we might be filled with the greatness of our Lord and Savior, that we will go to God for all of our needs, because He is the supplier, that we recognize Him for who He has been and who He has promised to be in the midst of all that we go through. The devil comes only to steal, kill, confuse, deposit fear and destroy all that God has for us. God comes to give and the devil comes to take. **(John 10: 10) "The thief cometh not, but for to steal, and to kill, and to destroy: I am come that they might have life, and that they might have it more abundantly."**

I pray right in this moment that no matter where we are, no matter what we are going through that we would confidently know that God will lead us, guide us, carry us and give us anything that we need to continue to press forward for Him. I pray right now **(Ps.20: 1-2) "The LORD hear thee in the day of trouble; the name of the God of Jacob defend thee; Send thee help from the sanctuary, and strengthen thee out of Zion."**

I pray that we do nothing on our own, but that we call to our Father that He might direct our steps and guide our ways, that He might protect us from the enemy. To God be the Glory!

Additional References: Exodus 3:21, Deuteronomy 15:13, Philippians 4:13, Ps.37: 23,73:24

Reflections:

The Cracks

*T*hank God for the breath of life. I breathe in the grace and mercy of my Father and exhale condemnation, insecurity and low-self esteem. I thank God for the purpose He has for me. He has purposed me to do great things. I thank Him for the supernatural abilities that I have in the natural. **(2Samuel 22:2-4) "The LORD is my rock, and my fortress, and my deliverer; The God of my rock; in him will I trust: he is my shield, and the horn of my salvation, my high tower, and my refuge, my saviour; thou savest me from violence. I will call on the LORD, who is worthy to be praised: so shall I be saved from mine enemies."**

What happens when you feel like you are standing on solid ground and then all of a sudden the ground begins to crack and the crack keeps getting bigger and bigger, the things that you thought you needed most begin to roll right past you falling into what used to be a crack and now is a big hole. There you are standing on the edge of a big hole looking down at all the things you thought were the most important things in your life. LOOK DOWN NO MORE. KNOW that this is the power of God working in your life. It is GOD coming to show you His power and the greater things He has for you. God begins to remove all the things that you thought you needed. God has to remove all the things we rely on until we rely solely on Him for everything.

I pray that we would LOOK UP! LOOK UP and focus

on Him, not what we are losing. **(Ps.121: 1-2a) "I will lift up mine eyes unto the hills, from whence cometh my help. My help cometh from the LORD."** God is building a new foundation. He is rebuilding us and making us brand new. In our newness we will only be able to appreciate newness. **(2Corinthians 5: 17) "Therefore if any man be in Christ, he is a new creature: old things are passed away; behold, all things are become new."**

I pray that we would celebrate not what we lost, but the greater things that God has for us, that we would LOOK UP until when we look down the hole exists no more. When we are concentrating on what's up, our praises go up and blessings come down, we are blessed. God is meeting our needs while our heads are lifted to Him; He's filling in the hole with His love, peace, joy and strength to keep us from falling in the hole after what we thought we needed. He is creating a foundation that is all about Him.

I pray that we confidently know that God can do anything. He gives us all that we need when we are looking to Him for it. I pray that as we concentrate on Him, He is concentrating on us. To God be the Glory!

Additional References: Ps.16:11, 27:8, 46:10, Matthew 11:28, Jude 24

Reflections:

Use Them For His Glory

I am thankful that I have a God who has offered me all things not because of anything I have done, but for what Jesus has done for me. His grace and mercy is new every morning. I praise, exalt, worship, adore, and love MY GOD. The one who saved me from myself, the one who brought me out of circumstances that could have killed me, that brought me through circumstances that almost made me lose my mind, the one who held me when no one else deemed me worthy or knew how much I needed it, the one who sees my weaknesses when every one else thinks I'm strong, I am NOTHING without Him.

I can do NOTHING without Him. I am only a vessel willing to be used, I am a body carrying around things that He can use: I have a mind willing to be filled with His thoughts, I have a heart willing to love as He loves, I have ears ready to hear His directions, I have arms willing to give hugs so that people can feel His comfort, and I have a mouth to preach the gospel. I have these things because He gave them to me, so I use them for the reasons He gives me to use them. You also have these things. What are you using them for?

I pray that we be in complete obedience to His will, that we realize apart from Him we are and can do nothing. **(Exodus 13: 9-10) "And it shall be for a sign onto thee upon thine hand, and for a memorial between thine eyes, that the Lord's law may be in thy mouth; for with a strong hand hath the Lord brought thee out of Egypt.**

You must keep this ordinance at the appointed time year after year."

I pray: that we understand and appreciate where God has brought us from, that we receive peace and freedom from the place we have been delivered from, or are being delivered from, because it is that place that God will take us back to so that others can be delivered.

I pray that we get ready to be used by God at His appointed time. **(Deuteronomy 10: 12-13) "And now, O Israel, what does the Lord your God ask of you but to fear the Lord your God, to walk in all His ways, to love Him, to serve the Lord your God with all your heart and with all your soul and to observe the Lord's commands and decress that I am giving you today for your own good."**

I pray: that every step we take be a closer step to God's will for our life, that we seek Him for direction and begin to walk in that direction, that nothing hinders us, that our mind is clear of confusion brought on by our flesh and/or other people's flesh. **(Ephesians 5: 6-10) "Let no one deceive you with empty words, for because of such things God's wrath comes on those who are disobedient. Therefore do not be partners with them. For you were once darkness, but now you are light in the Lord. Live as children of light (for the fruit of the light consists in all goodness righteousness and truth) and find out what pleases the Lord."**

I pray: that we not get so caught up in our plans and other people's plans for us until we have complete direction from God, that we see people through the eyes of God and not our natural eye, that we do nothing to glorify ourselves, but everything to glorify God. To God be the GLORY!

Additional References: Deuteronomy 5:24, Ps.21:5, Isaiah 6:3

Reflections:

God, I Want:

Your desire to be my desire
You in every area of my life
To know You intimately
To be committed to You
To love what You love and hate what you hate
To be led and guided by You
To depend on You for everything that I need
To be honest with You
To speak boldly before You
To crave You
To be deeply acquainted with You
To perceive and recognize everything about You
To understand You in every way
To be familiar with Your voice
To be changed and made more like You daily
To be the best You created me to be
To have the heart of a servant
To serve
To be humble
To grow in You daily
To be wise, fill me up with Your wisdom
To be changed from the inside out
To grow and develop that I might be more like Christ
To be processed
To be a disciple of Christ
To be used for Your Glory
To be molded and shaped in the likeness of Christ
To develop all that I need to stay in Your presence
To make every effort to grow spiritually
To exist for Your purpose
To have Your word cause miracles to happen in my life
Your word to occupy my mind and body
I hunger, yearn, and thirst for You above anything else.

Are You Under Attack?

What a wonderful and glorious God we serve. As I sit in His presence I am consumed with peace, filled with joy, love is wrapped around me and I am prepared to face all obstacles. I give Him the sacrifice of praise because it is through my praise that my intimacy with Him grows. I submit myself to Him each day and ask for His will to be done in my life because it is not about me but all about Him. **(Ps. 33:1) "Rejoice in the LORD, O ye righteous: for praise is comely for the upright."**

I pray that we would submit to His will and His way that we would surrender to His plan which is the best plan for our lives. He wants to give us exceedingly, abundantly above according to HIS RICHES AND GLORY, not ours.

I pray: that we would know who we are and what we can accomplish when we submit to Him, that we would not allow ourselves to be attacked by the enemy, that we would use our sword to respond to Him. Is he telling you what you aren't, what you can't do, Is he confusing you with his lies?

I pray: that we know his voice, that we recognize the difference between him and God, that every time we hear his voice we respond to him with the words, the force, and the power of our GOD, that we know that He can accomplish nothing in our life if we stay focused on accomplishing what God has already predestined us to accomplish, that we resist the devil and watch him flee, that we tell the devil who we are in Christ. (Matthew 5: 13a, 14a) "Ye are the salt of the earth. Ye are the light of the world" (John 1: 12) "But as many as received him, to them gave he power to become the sons of God, even to them that believe on his name" (Romans 6: 18) "Being then made free from sin, ye became the servants of righteousness." (Romans 8: 14&17) "For as many as are led by the Spirit of God, they are the sons of God. And if children, then heirs; heirs of God, and joint-heirs with Christ; if so be that we suffer with him, that we may be also glorified together." (2Corinthians 5:17) "Therefore if any man be in Christ, he is a new creature: old things are passed away; behold, all things are become new."

When the devil tries to tell you who you were, tell him yes I was but look at me now. Take a good look because I'm going to keep getting better with the strength, love and comfort of my Lord and Savior Jesus Christ. (Ps.34: 15) "The eyes of the LORD are upon the righteous, and his ears are open unto their cry." The devil is defeated and with the sword in our hand and His words in our mouth, we have the POWER! To God be the Glory!

Additional References: 2Corinthians 2:10-11,10:5, 1Peter 5:8-9

Reflections:

Are You Under Attack Pt2?

Glorify the Lord! The Lord is worthy! It is Him who is worthy to be praised. He is worthy to be glorified! **(Ps. 18: 1-3a) " I will love thee, O LORD, my strength. The LORD is my rock, and my fortress, and my deliverer; my God, my strength, he LORD is my rock, and my fortress, and my deliverer; my God, my strength, in whom I will trust; my buckler, and the horn of my salvation, and my high tower. I will call upon the LORD, who is worthy to be praised."**

I pray: that we stand firm on the sword that our Father has given us, that we get our identity from Him, that we take on the identity that God has predestined us for, that we know His will and purpose for our life, that we accept our inheritance. **(Galatians 4: 7) "Wherefore thou art no more a servant, but a son; and if a son, then an heir of God through Christ." (Ephesians 2: 13) "But now in Christ Jesus ye who sometimes were far off are made nigh by the blood of Christ."** Let us serve notice on the devil and let him know that we are standing in agreement with our God for our life. We agree with all that He has for us and from this moment on we are moving towards and in our destiny.

(John 10:27) "My sheep hear my voice, and I know them, and they follow me" (Colossians 3: 2-3) "Set your affection on things above, not on things on the earth. For ye are dead, and your life is hid with Christ in God." I pray that we will not allow Satan to destroy our today with what we did and repented for yesterday. We are new creatures in Christ. He has forgiven us and set us on a path for greatness. The reason that we should not give our past mistakes any thought is to glorify God for His grace and mercy, to glorify God for the changes He has made in us, to glorify God for His presence in all that we go through, to glorify God that we didn't lose our mind, kill ourselves, or get killed in the midst of our sin but that we are still here with a testimony and a celebration.

(1Peter 2: 4-5) **"To whom coming, as unto a living stone, disallowed indeed of men, but chosen of God, and precious, Ye also, as lively stones (Christ, the foundation of the church and of the hopes of his people) are built up a spiritual house, an holy priesthood, to offer up spiritual sacrifices (of a broken heart and a contrite spirit, mingled with the incense of thanksgiving and praise), acceptable to God by Jesus Christ."** We are God's workmanship; let us stand before Him asking for His will to be done in our lives. Let us praise Him for change, thank Him for the process and fight the devil with the sword God has given us each and every time He tries to put his hand in the midst of the pot in which we are being molded in. To God be the Glory!

Additional References: Ephesians 2:13, Mark 11:24, Ps.50:15

Reflections:

Prayer

❧

Prepare your hearts for prayer, clear your minds for purity, and rest in this moment knowing that the next one will be a moment of expectancy for greatness to evolve.

*H*eavenly Father,

We come to You in agreement that there is nothing greater than You, not one person or thing. We come to You with our mouth full of praise, we thank You for being a need meeter and a heart fixer, and we bless Your name because we realize that You are worthy of our all. Father forgive us when we fall short, forgive us when we go our own way thinking that it will be faster, greater and/or better. Forgive us for all the times that we didn't trust You and place our faith in You. We repent Father for all the times we strayed to look for another way.

We thank You that You unconditionally love us and we ask that You continue to do so. We ask that You continue to love us in spite of ourselves, we ask that You continue to draw near to us, we would not be here if we were not trying to draw closer to You. We know that nothing is an accident, nothing happens for nothing but everything happens for a reason and we seek not the reason on this day we just take in all that You are offering us and give You all that is on our heart. We truly love and adore You and are confident that there is no one or nothing like You.

We thank You in advance not for what You have done but for who You are. You are all that we need and Lord when we fall short of realizing that remind us, remind us of what You've done, remind us of who You are and remind us of Your unconditional love. In Jesus' name we thank You. Amen.

To God be the Glory!

Reflections:

God's Presence

*T*will bless the Lord at all times and His praises shall
continually be in my mouth. I'm thankful that I have
a best friend. He is a friend that gives me all that I need. I
am thankful that He has supplied me with the knowledge
and understanding of Him. **(1Ch 23:30a) "And to stand
every morning to thank and praise the LORD"**

I pray: that we would seek more and more of Him that
we might be set free from ourselves, that we will become
liberated to be and feel worthy of not only Him but worthy
to do all things through Him, that we would trust Him for all
that we need, that no need go unmet, that we seek Him to
supply all of our needs, that we seek Him when we have
questions, wants, desires and/or confusion. **(Joshua. 1: 5)
"There shall not any man be able to stand before thee all
the days of thy life: as I was with Moses, so I will be with
thee: I will not fail thee, nor forsake thee."**

I pray: that we know that whenever, wherever and how-
ever we need Him, He will give us His attention, that we see
our importance in His eyes even if and when we don't see it
in our own and or in others, that we have a clear vision of
what God's purpose is for our life, that we focus on His call
or focus on finding out what His call is for our life. He
knows us better than we know ourselves and His desire is to
give us exceedingly abundantly above all that we could ever
ask for. He knows what we need and I pray that we draw

close to Him that He might fulfill our needs and give us peace while He is doing it. **(Ps. 139: 1-5) "O LORD, thou hast searched me, and known me. Thou knowest my downsitting and mine uprising, thou understandest my thought afar off. Thou compassest my path and my lying down, and art acquainted with all my ways. For there is not a word in my tongue, but, lo, O LORD, thou knowest it altogether. Thou hast beset me behind and before, and laid thine hand upon me."**

I pray that we remain patient as we lift our desires and our needs up to Him. He knows us and He knows how to give us what is best for us.

I pray: that we remain patient because it is in that patience where our faith is built and it is because of that faith that God will build us, that we want what God wants for us because we can only ask for what we see. but God will give us what He knows we deserve which goes beyond our sight. To God be the Glory!

Additional References: Ps.46:11, Romans8:31,37, Joshua 3:7, Deuteronomy.31:8,23, Matthew 28:20, 2Timothy 4:17, Isaiah 41: 10-14, Jeremiah 12:3

Reflections:

Your Anointed Tears

*T*will bless the Lord at all times and His praises shall continually be in my mouth. He is great and greatly I will praise Him. I love Him and thank Him for who and what He is in my life. He is faithful and He is just and I thank Him for His grace and mercy **(Ps. 119:169) "let my cry come near before thee, O Lord: give me understanding according to thy word." (Ps. 9: 1-2) "I will praise thee, O LORD, with my whole heart; I will shew forth all thy marvellous works. I will be glad and rejoice in thee: I will sing praise to thy name, O thou most High."**

I pray: that we would trust God with our whole heart, that we would depend on Him to meet our emotional needs. God is faithful and He unconditionally loves us. When we are down He can pick us up. When we are hurt He can heal us and when we cry He catches every tear. **(Luke 7: 37-38) "And, behold, a woman in the city, which was a sinner, when she knew that Jesus sat at meat in the Pharisee's house, brought an alabaster box of ointment, And stood at his feet behind him weeping, and began to wash his feet with tears, and did wipe them with the hairs of her head, and kissed his feet, and anointed them with the ointment."**

I pray that we would go to Him when we need to release our tears and wash Him with everyone of them. **(Luke 7: 44-50) "And he turned to the woman, and said unto Simon, Seest thou this woman? I entered into thine** house, thou gavest me no water for my feet: but she hath washed my feet with tears, and wiped them with the hairs of her head. **Thou gavest me no kiss: but this woman since the time I came in hath not ceased to kiss my feet. My head with oil thou didst not anoint: but this woman hath anointed my feet with ointment. Wherefore I say unto thee, Her sins, which are many, are forgiven; for she loved much: but to whom little is forgiven, the same loveth little. And he said unto her, Thy sins are forgiven. And they that sat at meat with him began to say within themselves, Who is this that forgiveth sins also? And he said to the woman, Thy faith hath saved thee; go in peace."** Our tears are our source of compassion.

I pray that through them, God will use our tears to make us even more compassionate. Our tears are our gratitude for God for changing our lives and taking it from our hands and manifesting it in His. To God be the Glory!

Additional References: Isaiah 61:3, John 3:16

Reflections:

His Name

*W*hat a mighty God we serve! He is worthy of all the praises. I sit as a hungry servant bowing at His feet breathing in the breath of a new life exhaling the death of the flesh. No flesh shall Glory in anything that I say or do because it is only by His grace and mercy that accomplishments can be written under my name. **(Ps. 96:4) "For the LORD is great, and greatly to be praised: he is to be feared above all gods."**

I pray: that we would recognize the power that we have in His name, that we would walk in the authority that He has given us, that we would take a moment and call His name, just say Jesus! Jesus! Jesus, can you feel it? Can you feel the peace that you get just from saying His name? It is His name that we can call out and a presence of love, peace and comfort rest in us. We don't have to be loud, just let it be a soft whisper. Jesus. , Can you feel His presence as you welcome Him in. As you call Him in, as you invite Him in a peace sits in your heart, His arms wrap around you. Jesus. Can you feel the emptiness in your body as everything that is not like Him has been removed? He's refreshing you with everything that is of Him, strength, peace, joy and calmness. Can you feel the burdens being lifted as you surrender them to Him? Jesus. Can you feel your mind being cleared of confusion and chaos? Jesus. Can you feel the weight being lifted from your shoulders? Jesus. Can you feel your body being filled with strength?

I pray that whatever we need: comfort, peace, security, joy, fulfillment, direction, attention, unconditional love, completeness, or a higher place in God, that we call on that name Jesus!

I pray that we allow ourselves to get what He offers in His name. Call Him His number is never busy, He'll never put us on hold, He'll never not answer, He may not give us the answer we want, but He'll always give us the answer we need. **(Lamentations 3: 23b-36) "Great is thy faithfulness. The LORD is my portion, saith my soul; therefore will I hope in him. The LORD is good unto them that wait for him, to the soul that seeketh him. It is good that a man should both hope and quietly wait for the salvation of the LORD." Call Him. (Philippians 4: 19) "But my God shall supply all your need according to his riches in glory by Christ Jesus." CALL HIM! (Ps. 16:11) "Thou wilt shew me the path of life: in thy presence is fulness of joy; at thy right hand there are pleasures for evermore." CALL HIM! (Hebrews 13: 5b) "for he hath said, I will never leave thee, nor forsake thee."** Call Him! Take a deep breath and as you exhale call His name. To God be the Glory!

Additional References: Ps.31:24, Job13:15, 1Peter 1:13,21, Genesis 28:15, Isaiah 41:10

Reflections:

We Can Find It, In Him

(Ps. 100: 1-3) "Make a joyful noise unto the LORD, all ye lands. Serve the LORD with gladness: come before his presence with singing. Know ye that the LORD he is God: it is he that hath made us, and not we ourselves; we are his people, and the sheep of his pasture." (Ps. 103: 1-5) "Bless the LORD, O my soul: and all that is within me, bless his holy name. Bless the LORD, O my soul, and forget not all his benefits: Who forgiveth all thine iniquities; who healeth all thy diseases; Who redeemeth thy life from destruction; who crowneth thee with lovingkindness and tender mercies; Who satisfieth thy mouth with good things; so that thy youth is renewed like the eagle's."

*T*pray that we allow God to make us strong when we are weak that we hold on to what we hear more than we concentrate on what we see. It is only when we hear a word from the Lord that we begin working our faith to trust and believe that if He said it, it shall be.

I pray that God would strengthen us for every journey. (2Corinthians 12:9) "And he said unto me, my grace is sufficient for thee: for my strength is made perfect in weakness. Most gladly therefore will I rather glory in my infirmities, that the power of Christ may rest upon me."

I pray: that we stay focused regardless of the clouds,

that we keep our ears open, that when we can't see past the tears, that we leave our heart with Him when it has been broken and shattered in several pieces, that we rest and repent in His arms after we have exhausted ourselves doing it our way, that we stand strong and worship Him, but when we can't stand and worship, we kneel and pray before Him that He might strengthen us to get back up again. He is our strength, trust, hope and peace and with Him all things are possible. To God be the Glory!

Additional References: Jeremiah 28:7,Joshua 1: 9, Hebrews 4: 16, Ephesians 3:17-19

Reflections:

What Is It That You Think?

I worship Him because He is worthy and I'm forever grateful for all He has done and continues to do. He is worthy! **Ps.118: 21) "I will praise thee: for thou hast heard me, and art become my salvation."**

What is it that you think? In Proverbs it says a man's mind plans His ways but God directs His steps. What is your mind planning for you, what do you think about yourself? Your mind is a battlefield, which is what Satan is after. If He can control what we think about ourselves then He can determine our joy and our peace. The Bible says whatever a man thinketh so is he. Are we still thinking about our mistakes? God's mercies are new every morning; it is Satan that won't let us forgive others and/or ourselves. What is in your mind? Ask yourself what is it that you think about yourself? Does the devil have control of your mind? God has made promises to you. Are you walking confidently believing for them or did the devil tell you why you couldn't have them. Is your mind set on what things look like or is your mind set on what God has promised you **(Proverbs 3: 5) "Trust in the LORD with all thine heart; and lean not unto thine own understanding."**

I pray: that our mind is focused on God, that we leave no room for Satan in our mind, that we hold on to God's promises and when Satan comes to tell us what we can't, what we won't or what we are not capable of, that we stand strong on the word. We are the salt of the earth, we are the light of the world, we are fearfully and wonderfully made, fight for your mind, allow Satan no space in your mind. We are far more precious than rubies, we are here to birth what God has predestined us to birth. Satan wants to stop us from birthing. He is after our potential.

I pray: that we give him no area in our mind, that we keep our mind stayed on God, that we have a clear revelation of what God created us to be, that we walk and not faint, live and not die, that we open our mind to all that God has for us and rebuke the spirit of confusion, chaos, disappointment, and fear. (**Exodus14: 13-14**) **"And Moses said unto the people, Fear ye not, stand still, and see the salvation of the LORD, which he will shew to you to day: for the Egyptians whom ye have seen to day, ye shall see them again no more for ever. The LORD shall fight for you, and ye shall hold your peace."**

I pray that we allow God to be our sustainer, direction, strength, hope, peace and best friend. (**Deuteronomy 32: 3-4**) **"Because I will publish the name of the LORD: ascribe ye greatness unto our God. He is the Rock, his work is perfect: for all his ways are judgment: a God of truth and without iniquity, just and right is he." To God be the Glory!**

Additional References: Job13: 15, Jeremiah 17: 7-8, Isaiah 12:2-4, 26:4, 30: 15

Reflections:

Glorify Him

～

I pray that we would glorify God. He is worthy! I empty myself and ask God to fill me. It is not about me but it is all about Him. It is all about being lead by the Holy Spirit to do all that God has called me to do. God is good and worthy to be praised, magnified, and glorified.

(Habakkak 3:3b-4a) "His glory covered the heavens, and the earth was full of his praise. And his brightness was as the light."

I pray that we would re pre sent Christ in all that we say and do. **(Ephesians 4:29) "Let no corrupt communication proceed out of your mouth, but that which is good to the use of edifying, that it may minister grace unto the hearers."**

We all have a purpose in life and that purpose is to glorify God. We need to ask ourselves a few questions. Do you think our lack of confidence in our self glorifies God? When in His word He is clear about who we are: YOU ARE FEARFULLY AND WONDERFULLY MADE, YOU ARE MORE PRECIOUS THAN RUBIES, AND YOU ARE THE HEAD AND NOT THE TAIL. Do you think that having a foul mouth, gossiping, lying and/or haughty behavior glorifies God.

When His word says: **(Proverbs13: 3) "He that keepeth his mouth keepeth his life: but he that openeth wide his lips shall have destruction." (Proverbs 17: 28) "Even** a fool, when he holdeth his peace, is counted wise: and he that shutteth his lips is esteemed a man of understanding." Do you think if we have an unclean house it glorifies God? When the word says: (Proverbs 31: 27-28) "She looketh well to the ways of her household, and eateth not the bread of idleness. Her children arise up, and call her blessed; her husband also, and he praiseth her." Do you think if we refuse to submit to our husband it glorifies God? When the word says: (Ephesians 5:22-23) "Wives, submit yourselves unto your own husbands, as unto the Lord. For the husband is the head of the wife, even as Christ is the head of the church: and he is the saviour of the body." Do you think it glorifies God when as a husband you don't love your wife? When the word says: (Ephesians 5: 25) "Husbands, love your wives, even as Christ also loved the church and he gave himself for it."

I pray: that we would put a glorify God check on our lives, that we ask the spirit to help US remove everything in our heart, mind and mouth that does not glorify God, that the Holy Spirit will convict us each and every time we do something that does not glorify God, that we walk in perfect peace, unconditional love and re pre sent and glorify God in all that we say and do. To God be the Glory!

Additional References: Ps.22:23, Ps.50:15, Isaiah 25:3, Matthew 5:16

Reflections:

Pray With Me:

Prepare your hearts for prayer, clear your minds for purity, and rest in this moment knowing that the next one will be a moment of expectancy for greatness to evolve.

Father God, we know You as Father and we thank You for being better to us than we have been to ourselves. We thank You that Your plan is greater than our plan. We lift You up and sing praises to Your name. We come to You in the mighty name of Jesus. We obediently seek after Your will for our lives. Lord we ask You to give us more grace, more grace to trust You, more grace to be patient in our wait.

Father, continue to strengthen us in every area of our lives, continue to give us peace that passes all understanding, hear our cry when we call out to You. We realize that we need You, we need You to guide us in the way in which we should go. Lord direct our steps that every step we take be a step closer to Your will and Your way for our lives.

Father, give us a mind of clarity, where no confusion shall lie, give us a heart that loves as You love, give us a soul that is in line with Your perfect will for our lives and give us eyes that stay focused on You, give us a clean heart, a right spirit and a renewed mind, give us an overflowing of blessings. Prosper us as You see fit. As You do mighty works in our lives, when the blessings are not able to be seen in the flesh, keep us Lord, keep us patient, keep us joyful, keep us focused on You, all the weapons that are formed against us let NOT one prosper. Speak wholeness into our lives. I bind the spirit of loneliness, confusion, selfishness, unforgiveness, haughtiness and depression. We bless Your name Father and we thank You in advance for what we know You will do in our lives. We thank You for Your favor. In the mighty name of Jesus Amen. To you Lord be the Glory!

Additional References: Ps.51: 10, Isaiah.40: 31, Romans 5:3, 8: 25, Ps.5: 3, Proverbs 3: 6

Reflections:

Choice

praise a worthy and awesome God. He is worthy to be praised. **(Hebrews 13:15) "By him therefore let us offer the sacrifice of praise to God continually, that is, the fruit of our lips giving thanks to his name."** I thank Him for His love, for loving me even when I was doing the wrong things. God loved me and drew me closer to Him that I might have His mind and make decisions not based on me but based on Him. **(James 5:13) " Is anyone among you afflicted? He should pray. Is any merry? Let him sing psalms." I'm glad!**

I pray: that we make the choice to stand, walk and be obedient to the God who has promised to supply all of our needs, to never leave us or forsake us, to give us life more abundantly.

I pray: that we would re pre sent the God whom we worship and glorify in our lives, that we walk a walk that exemplifies Him regardless of our circumstances, that we would pick up our cross and carry it as He did so that we may do greater things than even Jesus did. We have a cross and that cross is that one thing that stands in the way of God's promises and us. God has made us personal promises, but sometimes to get to those promises we have to carry our cross. So, I pray that we would carry it as Jesus did and keep on pressing forward. **(Deuteronomy 28: 1-2) "And it shall come to pass, if thou shalt hearken diligently unto the** voice of the LORD thy God, to observe and to do all his commandments which I command thee this day, that the LORD thy God will set thee on high above all nations of the earth: And all these blessings shall come on thee, and overtake thee, if thou shalt hearken unto the voice of the LORD thy God." God gives us choices! We can choose to live by His word or by our own rules. If we have had just a taste of God's grace, mercy, love, joy and/or goodness we will have an appetite for the food of the word. Hunger after Him. The word can fill us up until we are overflowing. We need NOTHING else but what God is giving us. Even when what we hear from God doesn't seem to taste good we must recognize that it is good for us. We have to choose to follow God regardless of ourselves; we have to choose beyond our thoughts, beyond our experiences and or beyond the people who surround us. **(Matthew7: 26-27) "And every one that heareth these sayings of mine, and doeth them not, shall be likened unto a foolish man, which built his house upon the sand: And the rain descended, and the floods came, and the winds blew, and beat upon that house; and it fell: and great was the fall of it."** I pray that we would not only choose to hear the word but that we would choose to live by the word as our guide line for life. To God be the Glory!

Additional References: Luke 11:28, Acts 15:7, Joshua 24:15

Reflections:

Put Off and Put On

⟨⟩

*G*lory be to God who has yet given me another day. Bless His name. He is awesome. I thank Him for continued comfort, blessings that continue to flow and a magnified anointing. Praise Him because He is worthy. I'm thankful beyond measure that God loves me in spite of myself. **(1Peter1:3) "Blessed be the God and Father of our Lord Jesus Christ." (Jeremiah 17:14) "Heal me, O Lord, and I shall be healed; save me, and I shall be saved, for thou art my praise."**

I pray that we put off the old man and put on the new **(Ephesians 4: 22-25,31-32) "That ye put off concerning the former conversation the old man, which is corrupt according to the deceitful lusts. And be renewed in the spirit of your mind; And that ye put on the new man, which after God is created in righteousness and true holiness. Wherefore putting away lying, speak every man truth with his neighbour: for we are members one of another Let all bitterness, and wrath, and anger, and clamour, and evil speaking, be put away from you, with all malice: And be ye kind one to another, tenderhearted, forgiving one another, even as God for Christ's sake hath forgiven you." (Romans 12: 2-3) "And be not conformed to this world: but be ye transformed by the renewing of your mind, that ye may prove what is that good, and acceptable, and perfect, will of God. For I say, through**

the grace given unto me, to every man that is among you, not to think of himself more highly than he ought to think; but to think soberly, according as God hath dealt to every man the measure of faith."

One way to glorify God is by being like Jesus. God has given every moment of our lives to us. He has given us the opportunity to glorify Him so that people will want what we have. Let them see the Jesus in You. There are a lot of hurting people in this world and one of our duties is to show them the ultimate healer. Jesus loves sinners such as us so we must also love others and ourselves. LOVE THE HELL right out of them.

I pray: that we identify the gift God has given us, that we walk in the anointing He has given us, that we walk in the greatness that He has predestined for us, and when we look in the mirror, we see all that God sees in us, and if you can't see it today, we continue to draw to Him until He reveals it to us.

I pray that we look in that mirror everyday and ask God to continue to reveal to us who He thinks we are and what He has predestined us to do for such a time as this. I pray that through us people will be led to Him because we are showing them the beauty of holiness. To God be the Glory!

Additional References: Matthew 23:2, Romans 12: 2, 4-8, Jonah 3: 5, John 3:5, Ezekial 36:25-27

Reflections:

The Deeper Life

∽

*P*raise Him with a heart of thanksgiving. **(Ps. 64: 10)** **"The righteous shall be glad in the LORD, and shall trust in him; and all the upright in heart shall glory."**

I pray: that we all set SAIL FOR THE DEEPER LIFE, that we abandon ourselves to the care of a MIGHTY GOD, that we have joy in the midst of our accomplishments and even in our uncomfortable circumstances, that we praise God for giving us all the tools we need to get through, that we run the race until He accomplishes what He has already predestined to accomplish through us.

If everything could be easily accomplished then we wouldn't need God. It's the hard things, the things that we seek God for additional strength, the things that require us to empty ourselves and need more of God, the things that we seek God in need of His guidance, the things that when it's over we feel deserving of and appreciative of, these are the things in which we see His greatness. It is the hard times that when it's over we feel worthy of the rewards. God rewards the faithful, the hard working, the obedient, and the weak-the reliant on Him. **(Luke 5:4-7)** **"Now when he had left speaking, he said unto Simon, Launch out into the deep, and let down your nets for a draught. And Simon answering said unto him, Master, we have toiled all the night, and have taken nothing: <u>nevertheless at thy word I will let down the net</u>. And when they had this done,**

they inclosed a great multitude of fishes: and their net brake. And they beckoned unto their partners, which were in the other ship, that they should come and help them. And they came, and filled both the ships." (Emphasis mine)

I pray that we choose to live by the word, choose to put what we feel aside and do what He is calling us to do, what we feel in our heart is the best for us regardless of fear and the possibility of loss because it is in our heart that God speaks. I pray that we move in spite of what we think because God offers us exceedingly, abundantly and we shouldn't allow ourselves to settle for less because of what we see, because of what we have tried already, and/or because of what others have said. We should GO OUT INTO THE DEEP only because of what we have heard from God Himself, what He has clearly spoken into our heart.

I pray: that we choose to be obedient, that we choose to not get exhausted by our circumstances, that we choose to seek God for strength beyond our abilities, and that we choose to live on a deeper level. **(James 1: 22) "But be ye doers of the word, and not hearers only, deceiving your own selves."** To God be the Glory!

Additional References: Matthew17:27, John 2:5, 15:14, 21:6, Luke 6:46-48

Reflections:

Walk in It

I praise Him because He is great and worthy to be praised. I love Him because He has loved me in spite of myself. He has given me a second chance to be all that He has created me to be. **(Ps. 149:1) "Praise ye the Lord. Sing unto the Lord a new song, and his praise in the congregation of saints."**

I pray: that we will get a greater revelation daily of the direction in which our steps should take, that we would keep our mind stayed on Him, our heart filled with Him, our direction towards Him, our spiritual eyes focused on Him, our natural eye focused on the word, and our soul willing to do His perfect will for our lives.

I pray: that we would live like symbols of Jesus, that we would allow His ways to guide us, that everyday we will set greater goals for our character, that we might walk just like Jesus, that daily we will celebrate our God and who He is in our lives, that we might thank Him for all that He does through us and that we will continue to be open to be used by Him to do great things in the lives of everyone around us, as well as our own lives.

When we are close to Him, when we are obedient to Him, when we draw near to Him, it is in all of these ways that we experience the fullness of joy, the unspeakable peace and the power to endure whatever the day may bring. Stay close to Him and walk in that joy, walk in the comfort of His peace, walk in that power. **(John 10: 10) "The thief cometh not, but for to steal, and to kill, and to destroy: I am come that they might have life, and that they might have it more abundantly."** (Ps. 139:14a) **"I will praise thee; for I am fearfully and wonderfully made"** (Proverbs 3: 26) **"For the LORD shall be thy confidence."** (Hebrews 13: 5b) **"For he hath said, I will never leave thee, nor forsake thee."** So, don't leave Him, stay close and walk in YOUR POWER!

God has given us power to triumph over our enemies. He has equipped us to do great things. We just have to walk in the spirit and blow people's mind because of the grace that is on our lives. People can read the Bible everyday and know the word but until you can produce that word, that word means nothing. It falls on a heart of stone and deaf ears. Knowledge is not power, power is the application of knowledge. When we know what the word says we have to walk in it because it is there where our power lies. If we walk in responsibility for what we know in the word and walk in the word it becomes contagious to the people who refuse to move out of areas of jealousy, envy, backsliding, gossiping and lying. **(Romans 12:12) "Rejoicing in hope; patient in tribulation; continuing instant in prayer"** To God be the Glory!

Additional References: Genesis 17:1, Ps.23:4, Ephesians3:16

Reflections:

His Power/Our Power

〜

*O*ur God is an awesome God! He reigns from Heaven above with wisdom, power and His unconditional love. He is awesome and wonderful! There is none like Him. No one can touch our heart like our Father, the lover of our soul. He is the ultimate healer, lover and redeemer. He's all I need. He is everything. I am thankful that the Lord sees my heart. **(1Samuel 16: 7) "But the LORD said unto Samuel, Look not on his countenance, or on the height of his stature; because I have refused him: for the LORD seeth not as man seeth; for man looketh on the outward appearance, but the LORD looketh on the heart."** I am thankful that it is in Him that I find my peace regardless of my circumstances. **(John 16: 33) "These things I have spoken unto you, that in me ye might have peace. In the world ye shall have tribulation: but be of good cheer; I have overcome the world."**

I pray that we recognize that unlike man God never changes, He loves us the same today as He did yesterday. God does not judge us based on our accomplishments but based on who He is. He is love. **(James 1: 17) "Every good gift and every perfect gift is from above, and cometh down from the Father of lights, with whom is no variableness, neither shadow of turning." (Ephesians 3:18-19) "May be able to comprehend with all saints what is the breadth, and length, and depth, and height; And to**

know the love of Christ, which passeth knowledge, that ye might be filled with all the fulness of God."

I pray: that we draw to that power and love of Christ, that we see ourselves through His eyes, that when we need Him we crawl up into His loving arms and ask Him to breathe on us, to breathe into us life because all the life we have seems to be being sucked out of us by the cares of this world, that we would draw close to Him that we might receive all that we need to continue to do daily what He expects us to do and love on the people, He wants to see Him, through us. All we need is within us because He has prepared us for everything we need to do. We just have to make a decision to do it. God has done some marvelous things for us and it is our good and faithful service to allow Him to do some marvelous things through us. To God be the Glory!

Additional References: Romans 9:17, 2Timothy1:7, John 13:17, Mark 11:24

Reflections:

Stand Firm

*P*raise Him! Praise Him! Praise His name. I'm thankful that I have a slow dance partner, my God, I get a praise dance going with the lover of my soul and love on Him like no other because He is greater than any earthly person could ever be. In the midst of life He gives me a place of rest, peace and unspeakable joy.

He is worthy of my adoration, my worship, my praise, my obedience, my dedication and my honor. I can rock and cuddle in His arms of peace and comfort and feel a love above and beyond anything that I could ever imagine. A love that is complete, fulfilling and not based on me, but based on Him and what He has promised to give to me. **(Isaiah 25:1) "O Lord, Thou art God; I will exalt Thee, I will praise Thy name; for Thou hast done wonderful things;"**

I pray that we become over comers of evil, that we have a greater understanding of what it takes to defeat the devil. The devil wants us to have no joy, be confused, insecure, disobedient and lonely. He wants to see us lose as he did. He hates it when we praise God. We have taken over his job as worshipper. So, wave your hands in the air and praise God. Thank Him for His faithfulness. We have to stand firm in the word and know that the devil has no control. When he gives you negative thoughts combat them with the word. **(Ps. 91: 9-16) "Because thou hast made the LORD, which is my refuge, even the most High, thy habitation; there shall no** evil befall thee, neither shall any plague come nigh thy dwelling. For he shall give his angels charge over thee, to keep thee in all thy ways. They shall bear thee up in their hands, lest thou dash thy foot against a stone. Thou shalt tread upon the lion and adder: the young lion and the dragon shalt thou trample under feet. Because he hath set his love upon me, therefore will I deliver him: I will set him on high, because he hath known my name. He shall call upon me, and I will answer him: I will be with him in trouble; I will deliver him, and honor him. With long life will I satisfy him, and shew him my salvation." To God be the Glory!

Additional References: Exodus 14:13, Romans 5:2, 1Corinthians 16:13

Reflections:

Prayer -Worship Him

Prepare your hearts for prayer, clear your minds for purity, and rest in this moment knowing that the next one will be a moment of expectancy for greatness to evolve.

ord we thank You and we know that in Your word we are called to worship You and Lord we do worship You because You are worthy. We worship You Lord and we honor You. **(Ps. 29: 2) "Give unto the LORD the glory due unto his name; worship the LORD in the beauty of holiness" (Ps.10:17) "LORD, thou hast heard the desire of the humble: thou wilt prepare their heart, thou wilt cause thine ear to hear."**

Lord we desire to be people after Your heart as David was so Lord we come before You to worship because we know that it is through our worship that You see our heart. Lord we desire to know You that we might re pre sent You in all that we say and do. We love on You Lord on this day and thank You for all that You have done in our lives and we thank You in advance for all that You will use us to do in others lives.

We speak well of You Lord because it is through You that we are well, that we have a sound mind because our spirit is right with You, we have surrendered our will and our way and we desire for You to show us any area of our lives that has not been surrendered and help us to come to a place where we need more of You. In order to have more of You, we must make room in our lives by getting rid of the things that are unlike You. We worship You Lord! **(Exodus 15: 2) "The LORD is my strength and song, and he is become my salvation: he is my God."**

We praise You and we worship You, You are wonderful, You are perfect and You are the supplier of our every need. Humbly we bow down to You our majesty. We love You and honor You. To You Lord be the GLORY!

Reflections:

Growing With
His Direction in Faith

❧

Praise the Lord our God for His worthiness. Praise Him because there is none like Him. I praise Him for all that He has done in my life. **(Ps. 104: 1) "Bless the LORD, O my soul. O LORD my God, thou art very great; thou art clothed with honor and majesty." (Ps. 103: 1-2) "Bless the LORD, O my soul: and all that is within me, bless his holy name. Bless the LORD, O my soul, and forget not all his benefits." (Ps. 107: 1,21-22) "O give thanks unto the LORD, for he is good: for his mercy endureth forever. Oh that man would praise the LORD for his goodness, and for his wonderful works to the children of men! And let them sacrifice the sacrifices of thanksgiving, and declare his works with rejoicing."** HE IS WORTHY!

I pray that as our faith continues to grow and magnify that we look to the hills in which our help comes from. **(Mark 11: 22-24) "And Jesus answering saith unto them, Have faith in God. For verily I say unto you, That whosoever shall say unto this mountain, Be thou removed, and be thou cast into the sea; and shall not doubt in his heart, but shall believe that those things which he saith shall come to pass; he shall have whatsoever he saith. Therefore I say unto you, what things so ever ye desire, when ye pray, believe that ye receive them, and ye shall**

have them."

I pray that we would walk by faith, live by faith, believe by faith and believe that we receive by faith. It is because of our faith in God's word that we can walk confidently. **(Isaiah 40: 31) "But they that wait upon the LORD shall renew their strength; they shall mount up with wings as eagles; they shall run, and not be weary; and they shall walk, and not faint."** To God be the Glory!

Additional References: Mark 4:40, Galatians 3:2, Hebrews 11:6, James 1:3, 1Peter 1:7

Reflections:

His Love Endures Forever

*P*raise the Lord! I worship Him in spirit and in truth. I Glorify His name because it is a name that is above all names. Praise His Holy name! **(2Chronicles 7: 3) "And when all the children of Israel saw how the fire came down, and the glory of the LORD upon the house, they bowed themselves with their faces to the ground upon the pavement, and worshipped, and praised the LORD, saying, For he is good; for his LOVE endureth for ever."**

(Ps. 106: 1) " Praise ye the LORD. O give thanks unto the LORD; for he is good: for his mercy endureth for ever."

(1John 3:1) "Behold, what manner of love the Father hath bestowed upon us, that we should be called the sons of God: therefore the world knoweth us not, because it knew him not."

(Romans 8: 37-39) "Nay, in all these things we are more than conquerors through him that loved us. For I am persuaded, that neither death, nor life, nor angels, nor principalities, nor powers, nor things present, nor things to come, Nor height, nor depth, nor any other creature, shall be able to separate us from the love of God, which is in Christ Jesus our Lord."

(Deuteronomy 7: 7-9) "The LORD did not set his love upon you, nor choose you, because ye were more in number than any people; for ye were the fewest of all people:

But because the LORD loved you, and because he would keep the oath which he had sworn unto your fathers, hath the LORD brought you out with a mighty hand, and redeemed you out of the house of bondmen, from the hand of Pharaoh king of Egypt. Know therefore that the LORD thy God, he is God, the faithful God, which keepeth covenant and mercy with them that love him and keep his commandments to a thousand generations."

Aren't you thankful for His love? I am! I'm thankful for the height and depth of His love. God's love is new every morning. God's love, was there in the midst of every one of our circumstances. He was there with His protective arms wrapped around us. He was there in the good times and in the ones that seemed bad, but He walked us through them to make us stronger. Glorify Him, thank Him for HIS LOVE that ENDURES FOREVER. To God be the Glory!

Additional References: Ps.5:7, Ps.91:14, Isaiah 54:10

Reflections:

Die to Self

$\approx$

$\mathcal{H}$e's an Awesome Wonder, He's a Mighty God and He's worthy of all my praises. It is Him whom all accomplishments are because of. GLORY! GLORY! ALLELUIA. ! I sing praises, I speak praises and I think praises because I know that I have to praise Him for putting up with me. I want to thank Him for meeting me where I am, for showing up and showing off on my behalf. Thank you Lord for your unwavering, undying and unconditional love. **(Ps.107:1) "O Give thanks unto the Lord, for he is good: for his mercy endureth for ever."**

I pray: that God gives us a peace that passes all understanding, that in the midst of taking care of His business that we have peace. **(Jude 1: 1b-2) "to them that are sanctified by God the Father, and preserved in Jesus Christ, and called: Mercy unto you, and peace, and love, be multiplied."** There are times when we don't understand why God is doing what He is doing. But in the midst of it all I pray that we ask God for direction and peace until we receive it. Seek yea first the kingdom of God and everything we need will be added on to us. **(Hebrews 13: 5b)** God has said, **"For he hath said, I will never leave thee, nor forsake thee."**

I pray that we understand that we go through all that we go through for a reason. **(2Corinthians 4: 8-18) "We are troubled on every side, yet not distressed; we are perplexed, but not in despair; Persecuted, but not forsaken; cast down, but not destroyed; Always bearing about in the**

187

body the dying of the Lord Jesus, that the life also of Jesus might be made manifest in our body. For we which live are always delivered unto death for Jesus' sake, that the life also of Jesus might be made manifest in our mortal flesh. So then death worketh in us, but life in you. We having the same spirit of faith, according as it is written, I believed, and therefore have I spoken; we also believe, and therefore speak; Knowing that he which raised up the Lord Jesus shall raise up us also by Jesus, and shall present us with you. For all things are for your sakes, that the abundant grace might through the thanksgiving of many redound to the glory of God. For which cause we faint not; but though our outward man perish, yet the inward man is renewed day by day. For our light affliction, which is but for a moment, worketh for us a far more exceeding and eternal weight of glory; While we look not at the things which are seen, but at the things which are not seen: for the things which are seen are temporal; but the things which are not seen are eternal." DIE TO SELF.

I pray that everything we do be unto the Glory of God, that we DIE TO OUR FLESH and not take into account our sufferings. As Jesus suffered so shall we so that at the end of it all **(Romans 8: 28-29)" And we know that all things work together for good to them that love God, to them who are the called according to his purpose. For whom he did foreknow, he also did predestinate to be conformed to the image of his Son, that he might be the firstborn among many brethren."** I pray that peace rest on us as we carry our cross as our flesh is being crucified. I pray that our spirit be resurrected and we receive our VICTORY CROWN. TO GOD BE THE GLORY!

Additional References: Acts 1:8, Ephesians 3:17-19

Reflections:

Train Your Mind!

$\mathcal{A}$s you go from the deep sleep of the night to the rising of the sun that shines in on your face, God gently welcomes you into this fresh new day. As you lie there attempting to connect your mind and your body to move so that your day can begin, it is at that time before you say anything to anyone that you tell the lover of your soul "Good Morning." You awake the light that shines inside of you welcoming that light into this day to shine on the outside of you.

It is at that time that you spend the first few minutes of your day training your mind. Training your mind is essential to having a day filled with the joy of the Lord that keeps you strong. Training your mind to cast all of the cares of this day on Your God who has promised to be your ever present help. Training your mind to keep your focus on re pre sent ing Christ in all that you say and do. Training your mind to praise God in spite of the circumstances that come and go throughout your day.

As you make a conscious decision to keep your mind stayed on God and the training of your mind throughout your entire day, your feet touch the floor, the children are there with requests, the phone is ringing, the microwave is digging, and your husband needs. The day begins and circumstances are there readily awaiting for you to lose your focus.

The focus that you have from your morning training and

it is then that you pray your way through. It is then that you remind yourself that you are a child of the King, that the joy of the Lord is your strength, that you serve a God who is a way maker, that your Father has promised to never leave you or forsake you is near, that your provider has promised to provide for your every need, that your comforter has promised to be your dwelling place, that your helper has promised to be your ever present help in the time of trouble, that your peacemaker has promised to give you peace that surpasses all understanding, and that your healer has promised to be a heart fixer.

You victoriously pray yourself through the day with all of the training that your mind has been through. You spend your time moment-by-moment checking in with your Father who is always there. You'll end your day lying down as the sun goes away and darkness comes, with the light on the inside of you ready to give you rest. To God be the GLORY!

He Knows Our Desires

*M*y heavenly Father, the Father who loved me in spite of myself. I love Him, for He has set me free and liberated me. I worship the God who said I will **(Hebrews 13:5b) "for he hath said, I will never leave thee, nor forsake thee." (Ps.9: 1) "I will praise thee, O Lord, with my whole heart; I will shew forth all thy marvelous works."**

I pray that we stand firm on the promises that God has made to us, walk in who He told us we are, and who He is preparing us to be, seek Him for our place, position and peace. **(Exodus 15: 13) "Thou in thy mercy hast led forth the people which thou hast redeemed: thou hast guided them in thy strength unto thy holy habitation."**

I pray: that we would receive His unfailing love, it is that love that can meet all of our needs above and beyond anything that is imaginable to us, that we choose today His will and way because everything we need is in Him and He has promised in His word to give us the desires of our heart. **(1Samuel 16: 7b) "The LORD seeth not as man seeth; for man looketh on the outward appearance, but the LORD looketh on the heart."**

I pray that we understand the depth of love He feels for us that He looks beyond our faults, inadequacies and shortcomings and sees our heart. The heart that He gave us filled with the desires He gave us allow God to give you the desires of your heart because of His great love for you He knows what we need. If we try to satisfy our desires ourselves we get caught up in desires based on the world which can be far and few between, temporary, sinful and fall short of the complete pleasure we desire to receive from it. **(1John 2: 15-17)" Love not the world, neither the things that are in the world. If any man love the world, the love of the Father is not in him. For all that is in the world, the lust of the flesh, and the lust of the eyes, and the pride of life, is not of the Father, but is of the world. And the world passeth away, and the lust thereof: but he that doeth the will of God abideth for ever. "**

I pray: for the direction of our steps to be closer to God more and more daily, that we would walk in His perfect will for our lives, that we would seek Him first, that He rain on our field, breaking up the fowler ground that has been hardened by the cares of this world, that we choose to have a heart just like God's - to love like Him, care like Him, share like Him, and be like Him more and more daily, because the closer we get to Him the closer we will be to walking in overflowing blessings, walking in complete fulfillment, walking with abundant joy, walking in the anointing that He has placed on our life and walking with all our needs met and all our desires given on to us. To GOD be the GLORY!!!!

Additional References: Proverbs13:12, 10:24, 19:22, Exodus 15:9-19

Reflections:

192

He Is With Us

I praise Him for it is He who is worthy. It is His name that is above all names. I glorify and praise Him because He is worthy. Bless His name. Let us sit as hungry servants at His feet willing to submit to His will that is above our will. I ask Him to wash me, cleanse me of all my sin and protect me from all anxiety, give me a right spirit.

I am an obedient woman of God, with many imperfections but with a heart of GOD. Seeking to do His will for my life and stand in the midst of darkness so that people can see the light. The light in my eyes, the song in my voice, the strength in my stance, the greatness in my abilities and the confidence in my walk.

I offer myself to God as a living sacrifice, that He might use me to bring the hurting to salvation and to bring the religious to a greater love relationship with Him. God I give you the glory because it is not about me, and it is not about the people of and in this world, but it is all about You. **(Ps.150: 6) "Let everything that hath breath praise the Lord. Praise ye the Lord." (Ps. 47: 1-2,6) "O clap your hands, all ye people; shout unto God with the voice of triumph. For the LORD most high is terrible; he is a great King over all the earth. Sing praises to God, sing praises: sing praises unto our King, sing praises."**

I pray: that we all look for God in all people and see nothing of them but everything of God, that we would surrender our cares to God and not try to take things in our own hands, that we would not succumb to the pressures of this world, that we would not look at success based on the worlds standards, but that we would patiently rest in God, the God who promised to **(Hebrews 13:5b) "for he hath said, I will never leave thee, nor forsake thee."** Our God who is our need meeter and our ever present help. It is all about Him and it is in Him where we find the fullness of peace.

I pray that it is in Him that we put our complete trust knowing that He will guide us and take us through all that we go through, that we will not entertain doubt, fear, confusion and/or depression, but that we would look to the hills where our help comes from because our help comes from God.

I pray: that the Holy Spirit would silence all of the negative things that Satan brings to our remembrance and that the Holy Spirit would remind us daily of the promises of God, that God would increase our trust and patience in Him, that He would draw close to us and love us out of every circumstance. To God be the Glory!

Additional References: Romans 5:3, 8:25, 1Timothy 6:11, Ps.50:15, 55:17, 86:7

Reflections:

Prayer

∾

Pray with me knowing that we are asking for change, change that may not always feel good to our flesh.

*H*eavenly Father,

 I come to You in the mighty name of Jesus, praying for and with Your precious children, believing for character to be developed in us more and more daily, believing that each of us individually are on different levels going in different directions, I ask You God to deal with us all accordingly, deal with us based on our needs, but let us all see more of You in our life. We open our hearts to You, so that we might be totally open and transparent before You.

 Father, let us feel led to strip before You all that is displeasing to You, and allow You to cover us with Your righteousness. Help us daily to walk obedient and according to Your word even when we are In the midst of the people that have hurt us. Father, remove in us the spirit of unforgiveness, bitterness and resentment towards broken people who inflicted their brokenness on us that we will not inflict our brokenness on others.

 Father, we ask You to stop the cycle, using us. We ask that You build our self-esteem, so that we don't take everything that people say to us as a personal attack, let us be strong in You. Help us to walk in whom You say that we are, that we may have strength that shows on the inside and on the outside.

Father, cleanse our lips so that the words spoken from our mouths may be pleasing to You, cleanse our heart so that no unforgiveness, bitterness, or resentment will have a place there and give us a right spirit that seeks to serve You more and more daily. We hunger for more of You, for Your character to be showed off in all that we say and do. We bless Your name and thank You for not only what You have done, but also what You have planned to use us to do, for the furtherance of the kingdom. **(Ps. 150: 2) "Praise him for his mighty acts: praise him according to his excellent greatness."**

Thank You for the cooling streams that You have sent flowing through our lives in the overheated times. Thank You for the abundance of love that You shower us with in the midst of our dry spells, when everything in our lives is thirsty. Thank You for the dreams that by faith we believe are making the impossible, possible. Thank You for the vision that we couldn't have seen with our own eyes, but through Your unseen promises we will walk in confidence, believing and walking in those promises. We thank You for wrapping Your arms around us in the lonely times, for giving us direction in the blind times, for speaking confidence to us in the afraid times, for giving us weapons in the warfare times, and loving us in our unlovable times. We thank You for all times. **AMEN**

It's All About Him

〜

hat a wonderful day it is. God has yet bestowed upon us another day. I just want to love on Him today. I want to express my love for Him. I thank Him for the breath of life. Abundant life. Eternal life. I thank God that He has given me the choice to choose His will. I thank Him for being the lover of my soul and the Father who has made me whole. I thank Him for freedom on today, freedom to see myself through His mirror. I'm thankful that I can see beyond flesh right into the spirit. **(Hebrews 13:15-16) "By Him therefore let us offer the sacrifice of praise to God continually, that is, the fruit of our lips giving thanks to His name. But to do good and to communicate forget not: for with such sacrifices God is well pleased."**

I pray: that daily we will not judge people for who or what or where they are, that God would give us His spirit TO MEET people and GREET people where they are, the spirit that looks beyond flesh and ministers to the spirit, that we, like Him, be no respecter of persons, that we have a keen listening ear to share with people His word as He wants it shared, that we not be confused, fearful, depressed, lonely or selfish, that we will not carry the spirit of a gossiper, adulterer, drug addict, alcoholic, manipulative, self righteous, finger pointing or a bolster of self.

I pray: that moment-by-moment we recognize that we ARE NOTHING WITHOUT HIM, that God has made us brand new. It is NOT about us but it is ALL ABOUT HIM. RECOGNIZE where He has brought you? Think about where you could have been going, but look at where He is taking you. Glorify Him because we know that it is Him that made us whole or is making us whole. It is Him that brought us through, it is Him that is taking us to, and it is Him that has given us the vision of things that go beyond our biggest dreams. Glorify Him! Exalt His Name! Praise Him! It is all about Him, It is all about honoring Him in all that we say and do. What a wonderful feeling it is to feel His presence. I feel His presence resting on me as I write and give Him Honor. God rest on me and rest in me God. You are welcome, You are welcome in this place, in this broken vessel. You can abide in the presence of us God, we lift our heart, hands, and offer up praises to Your name. My prayer for us all **(Hebrews 13: 20-21) "Now the God of peace, that brought again from the dead our Lord Jesus, that great shepherd of the sheep, through the blood of the everlasting covenant, Make you perfect in every good work to do his will, working in you that which is wellpleasing in his sight, through Jesus Christ; to whom be glory for ever and ever. Amen."** TO GOD BE THE GLORY!

Additional References: Nehemiah:11, Mark 10:35, John 17:3

Reflections:

Equip US

〜〜

*P*raise Him on this day for He is worthy to be exalted. The Lord is good and greatly I will praise Him. He is faithful and I will bless His name above all names. **(Ps.34:1-2) "I will bless the LORD at all times: his praise shall continually be in my mouth."**

I pray: for all of us that we might be equipped by God to do great things. It is in the equipping that we are hard pressed, that when things are removed that we thought we needed and replaced by things that God wants us to have, the things that don't appear sometimes to be what we want but in our future in God's plan they are perfect. God has a plan for our lives and it is a bigger and better plan than we could ever plan for ourselves. He wants exceedingly, abundantly above all that we could ever ask for or think of. He wants us to look like we have favor on our lives. God takes us through the rough side of the road to take us to places people thought we would never make it to - but GOD. It is God who wants to be glorified by all that we go through and if we continue to lift Him up it is He who will lift us up right out of that circumstance. He is worthy.

I pray: that in all things we get understanding, that God would stay close by and listen to our cries for help when we need Him, that in all things we recognize that He is near. CALL HIM WHEN YOU NEED HIM. It is Him who sits by waiting to be asked for help. He predestined us to be where we are and it is Him who knows what we need to move to the next level that we might arrive to the place in which He wants us to get to. So we may not go through the drama, the trauma, the hills and the valleys for anyone else, but let us be willing on this day to go through it for Him. The lover of our soul who has proven that He is all we need, who has proven that He can do anything. Take a glance back at life - that's PROOF! He is able! **(Ps. 119: 9-17)" Wherewithal shall a young man cleanse his way? by taking heed thereto according to thy word. With my whole heart have I sought thee: O let me not wander from thy commandments. Thy word have I hid in mine heart, that I might not sin against thee. Blessed art thou, O LORD: teach me thy statutes. With my lips have I declared all the judgments of thy mouth. I have rejoiced in the way of thy testimonies, as much as in all riches. I will meditate in thy precepts, and have respect unto thy ways. I will delight myself in thy statutes: I will not forget thy word.**

Deal bountifully with thy servant, that I may live, and keep thy word. To God be the Glory!

Additional References: 2Chronicles 29:36, Ps.10:17, Isaiah 40:3

Reflections:

Be a Light

God is good and all the time He is good. I sing praises to His wonderful name. It is His name that is above all names. It is His name that I reverence. It is His name that gives me peace in my soul. I walk in His word, I live for His purpose, my will is His will and my desire is for Him to be LORD over every area of my life. **(2Chronicles 7: 3) "And when all the children of Israel saw how the fire came down, and the glory of the LORD upon the house, they bowed themselves with their faces to the ground upon the pavement, and worshipped, and praised the LORD, saying, For he is good; for his mercy endureth for ever."**

I pray: for newness in our lives, for us to walk in the new person that since we met Him, we have TURNED into, that we leave all the things that are not of Him, the things of this world, in the world. **(Matthew 5:13-14)** says you are **"the salt of the earth,"** says you are **"the light of the world."** I pray: that we would show off that light the light that God has made us, that we no longer live in darkness but in the light God has shown us - His light. He has showed us what He is and what we are in Him. Now it is up to us to show the world. **(Matthew 5:15-16) "Neither do men light a candle, and put it under a bushel, but on a candlestick; and it giveth light unto all that are in the house. Let your light so shine before men, that they may see your good works, and glorify your Father which is in heaven."**

I pray: that we would turn on the light, not a dim light that shows only a little light, but a BRIGHT light that shows our God in the midst of everything that we say and do, that in the midst of our circumstances, in the midst of the wilderness, in the midst of unbelievers we would reveal our God, and His word, that when we are faced with unbelievers/believers asking us how we are going to make it, we tell them "I can do all things through Christ who strengthens me."

I pray that when we are faced with unbelievers/believers asking us why we want a house/ car that is above what it looks like we can afford, we can tell them that we serve a God who promised to supply all of our needs and give us the desires of our heart.

I pray that when we are faced with unbelievers/believers asking us why we are always so happy, we can tell them it's because we have a solid foundation that's steady in the Lord and our happiness and joy are all found in Him. We can tell them that our joy is not predicated on success, material or people, but it is predicated on knowing who we are in our precious Lord. I pray that we let our light shine and win souls through that light. If we let our light shine as God has directed us to everyone in our presence who doesn't know Jesus will want to know Him. Introduce them through your light! To God be the Glory!

Additional References: Ps:43:2-4, John 12:35-36, John 12:46

Reflections:

Let Your Light Shine

〜

God alone is worthy of all my praises. He alone supplies all my needs. I exalt His name and thank Him that He has placed an anointing on my life to write and be filled with passion for doing His will.

I thank Him that it is Him that has equipped me to write with a desire to educate, edify and encourage. I bless His name. I sit as a hungry servant at His feet. I bow down humbly worshipping Him. **(Exodus 15:11b-12) "I will sing unto the LORD, for he hath triumphed gloriously: the horse and his rider hath he thrown into the sea. The LORD is my strength and song, and he is become my salvation: he is my God, and I will prepare him an habitation; my father's God, and I will exalt him."**

(John1:1-9) "In the beginning was the Word, and the Word was with God, and the Word was God. The same was in the beginning with God. All things were made by him; and without him was not any thing made that was made. In him was life; and the life was the light of men. And the light shineth in darkness; and the darkness comprehended it not. There was a man sent from God, whose name was John. The same came for a witness, to bear witness of the Light, that all men through him might believe. He was not that Light, but was sent to bear witness of that Light. That was the true Light, which lighteth every man that cometh into the world."

I pray that we boost on our God, that we share how great He is with others, that we explain our light to unbelievers that we let Him shine in our lives that our light will shine through our conversations and actions. To God be the GLORY!

Additional References: Daniel 12:3, 1John 1:7, Acts 13:47

Reflections:

Show Off Your Light

〜

I thank God for where He has brought me from and where He is taking me. His will is the best will for my life and I seek to do it daily. The Lord has shown me His light and He has shown me the light that He has put in my life. He has done this by showing me His word and revealing to me the many scriptures that give me a deeper understanding of His light in my life. I thank Him for showing me and giving me the peace and grace to share them with people as I receive a greater revelation of His goodness. **(Genesis 19:19) "Behold now, thy servant hath found grace in thy sight, and thou hast magnified thy mercy, which thou hast shewed unto me in saving my life."**

I pray for restoration that God will restore our soul and make us whole so that we may walk in His perfect will for our lives, that He gives us joy daily as we hold on firmly to His word and His light that He has given us so that we may have life and have it to the fullest. **(Ephesians 5:8-12) "For ye were sometimes darkness, but now are ye light in the Lord: walk as children of light: (For the fruit of the Spirit is in all goodness and righteousness and truth; Proving what is acceptable unto the Lord. And have no fellowship with the unfruitful works of darkness, but rather reprove them. For it is a shame even to speak of those things which are done of them in secret."**

I pray that God would give us the ability to talk to people not talk about people, that He would use us to be part of what draws people to Him, that God would shine through us that people might see what God has to offer them, that God would teach us the same mercy that He had for us, that we might have it for others, that God would teach us the same compassion He had for us, that we might give it to others. HUMBLE US FATHER that we might be more of a light for You. Let people see Him in our life, in our light, in the midst of our wilderness so that they may want Him or want more of Him. All people need is the desire and the Lord will meet them where they are the same way He met us. All He asks is that we introduce Him to them.

I pray that we would get past our religion, past our affliction, past our prejudice, past our thoughts and meet people where they are but before we go, we might have to take off a few things (our haughtiness, our conceited, condescending, holier than God himself, attitude) so that the light will shine better. **(Ephesians 5:20-21) "Giving thanks always for all things unto God and the Father in the name of our Lord Jesus Christ; submitting yourselves one to another in the fear of God."** To God be the Glory!!

<u>**Additional References:**</u> Acts 26:18, Romans 2:19, Romans 13:12

<u>**Reflections:**</u>

Praise Him

*T*hank God because His love endures forever and ever. I praise Him because He is worthy of all my praises. I worship Him because it is His light that continues to help me shine in the midst of darkness.

I exalt His name because He fulfills my every need, in spite of myself. I bless Him because He blesses me. I love Him because He chooses me. PRAISE HIM! PRAISE HIM! PRAISE HIM! **(Ps. 138:1) "I will praise thee with my whole heart: before the gods will I sing praise unto thee." (Ps. 84:2) "My soul longeth, yea, even fainteth for the courts of the LORD: my heart and my flesh crieth out for the living God." (John 4:23-24) "But the hour cometh, and now is, when the true worshippers shall worship the Father in spirit and in truth: for the Father seeketh such to worship him. God is a Spirit: and they that worship him must worship him in spirit and in truth."** WORSHIP HIM! WORSHIP HIM!

Tell Him how much you love Him. Tell Him how much you need Him.

I pray that we stand as true worshipers, that we stand worshiping the Lover of our Soul, that we get a slow dance with our ultimate partner, the partner who has promised to supply all our needs according to His riches, a partner who promised to **(Hebrews 13:5b) "for he hath said, I will never leave thee, nor forsake thee."** a partner who promised to give us the desires of our heart. **(Hebrews 13:15-16)** **"By him therefore let us offer the sacrifice of praise to God continually, that is, the fruit of our lips giving thanks to his name. But to do good and to communicate forget not: for with such sacrifices God is well pleased."** PLEASE HIM! PRAISE HIM! BLESS HIM! WORSHIP HIM! EXALT HIS NAME! TO GOD BE THE GLORY!

Additional References: Ephesians 5:19-20, Deuteronomy 10:21,Judges 5:3, Ps.7:17

Reflections:

Prayer

Pray with me knowing that we are asking for change, change that may not always feel good to our flesh.

*H*eavenly Father,

We glorify Your name. We praise You and we read in agreement with Your word. We read with confidence and understanding that there is no one greater than You.

Father, hear us calling You, hear us speaking to You, hear all that we lift up to You. We ask You God to enlarge our territory. You said in Your word You would give us double for our trouble. Some of us have been troubled for so long and we have drawn to You and now Lord we are ready. We are ready to receive all the things that You have promised us. Lord, if there is anything in any area of our lives that is unlike You we give You the authority right in this moment to remove it. REMOVE it that we might receive a greater portion of You.

Father, we thank You for change and we know that we are continuing to grow in You, for You and by You. We know that all that we are and everything that we desire is in You. REMOVE all that is not. If we have desires that are outside of Your will – REMOVE them Lord. We give you the authority to rest peacefully in us and we know in order for You to do that there are things that must be removed. REMOVE them. We honor you Lord and we bless Your name. We receive all that You have for us. In Jesus' name. To GOD be the Glory!

Reflections:

Focus on Him

I enter into God's presence with thanksgiving. I ask Him to rain on my field, break up the fowler ground and plant new seed, so, that I may be useful to do His will, to fulfill the call that He has placed upon my life. **(Romans 8:28) "And we know that all things work together for good to them that love God, to them who are the called according to his purpose."** Even when my heart is overwhelmed I trust Him and praise Him. **(Ps. 61:2) "I cry unto thee, when my heart is overwhelmed: lead me to the rock that is higher than I."**

I pray: for our focus to be stayed on Him, that we allow no circumstance, situation or person cause our focus to veer to the left or to the right but to constantly be stayed on Him, that we have a clear understanding that everything we do is on to God, that we believe by faith. Faith comes by hearing and hearing by the word of God. Our focus cannot be on what looks impossible. Nothing is impossible for our loving Father who desires to give us exceedingly, abundantly above all that we could ever ask for. I pray that our faith be bigger than anything that we desire. As we walk faithfully I pray that our focus be on the God who promised us our hearts desire.

I pray that if we are believing God for anything, that we focus on His word for everything. **(Ephesians 3:20) "Now unto him that is able to do exceeding abundantly above all that we ask or think, according to the power that wor-**

keth in us." I pray that we stand as obedient servants seeking to do His will. I pray that we walk in the word, that we stay focused on God's word He said if you draw to me, I'll draw to you. I pray that we would stand behind our forefathers and mothers. **(Hebrews 11:7-8,11,17,29,31) "By faith Noah, being warned of God of things not seen as yet, moved with fear, prepared an ark to the saving of his house; by the which he condemned the world, and became heir of the righteousness which is by faith. By faith Abraham, when he was called to go out into a place which he should after receive for an.** Through faith also **Sara herself received strength to conceive seed, and was delivered of a child when she was past age, because she judged him faithful who had promised. By faith Abraham, when he was tried, offered up Isaac: and he that had received the promises offered up his only begotten son. By faith they passed through the Red sea as by dry land: which the Egyptians assaying to do were drowned. By faith the harlot Rahab perished not with them that believed not, when she had received the spies with peace."** TO GOD BE THE GLORY!

<u>Additional References</u>: Isaiah 26:4, 40:31, Philippians 2:13, Ps.37:4-5, Joel2:25

<u>Reflections:</u>

His Grace Kept Me

〜

*O*ur God is an awesome God. RAIN God on my field, plant seed that can be usable by You . I bow down to worship You. **(Exodus 15:11) "Who is like unto thee, O LORD, among the gods? who is like thee, glorious in holiness, fearful in praises, doing wonders?"** You alone are worthy, You alone are able and You alone do I put my complete trust. I love You Lord not for what you've done but for who You are. My strong tower, my salvation, my strength, my hope and my song. So I sing praises to You with the song You have placed in my heart. I glorify Your name God.

I pray that our faith be magnified. Faith comes by hearing. **(2Corinthians 8:7-9) "Therefore, as ye abound in every thing, in faith, and utterance, and knowledge, and in all diligence, and in your love to us, see that ye abound in this grace also. I speak not by commandment, but by occasion of the forwardness of others, and to prove the sincerity of your love. For ye know the grace of our Lord Jesus Christ, that, though he was rich, yet for your sakes he became poor, that ye through his poverty might be rich."**

God is not going to make us rich or give us riches because we are poor. He is going to give them to us because of His grace. Faith comes by hearing the peace, that we should rest in believing that we can do all things THROUGH Him, believing that God is bigger than what we are believing for, believing that God is the supplier of all our

213

needs and gives us all the desires of our heart according to His will, believing that what ever we ask for in His name we shall receive. Grace comes by faith. Grace comes when we are walking in complete peace. God's grace will rest on us because of our peace in the midst of the unseen, but the heard. HEAR HIM! LISTEN! HE'S SPEAKING!

I pray that we walk in that grace, live by that grace, receive that grace. **(Ephesians 2:4-10) "But God, who is rich in mercy, for his great love wherewith he loved us, Even when we were dead in sins, hath quickened us together with Christ, (by grace ye are saved;) And hath raised us up together, and made us sit together in heavenly places in Christ Jesus: That in the ages to come he might shew the exceeding riches of his grace in his kindness toward us through Christ Jesus. For by grace are ye saved through faith; and that not of yourselves: it is the gift of God: Not of works, lest any man should boast. For we are his workmanship, created in Christ Jesus unto good works, which God hath before ordained that we should walk in them."**

This is why it is so important not to get caught up in others or ourselves. Because it is all about what God wants to use us to do. So, regardless of the person sitting next to us, the person laying next to us, the person we want laying next to us, the person living next door to us, the person working next to us, it is all about HIM. He gives us the mercy that allows us to see ourselves as He sees us. He desires for us to see ourselves with out the judgment of people, and without the judgment of ourselves.

RECEIVE HIS MERCY!!! We are no longer walking dead but we have been made alive by the word that is being planted in us.

I pray that we continue to allow God to mold us, shape us, create in us a clean heart and a right spirit, that we do everything on to Him. All of our works, make them God works. If He didn't tell you to do it, don't do it. If He didn't direct you to do it, don't do it. If He asked you to do it, do it, the word has given you direction - follow them. God has provided everything we need, so stop looking in the direction He didn't send you, stop concentrating on the things that are not of Him, let God be LORD OVER EVERY AREA OF YOUR LIFE and pray that He leaves not one area untouched. When you pray this, you must prepare yourself to be worked on and sometimes that work requires some pain. We can do all things through Christ, who will continually strengthen us through the process. To God be the Glory!!!!!!!!!!!!!!!!

Additional References: Ps.45:2, Proverbs 1:9

Reflections:

Great is the Holy One

$\approx\!\!\!\sim$

I love You, with all my heart. I love You. You are my shelter in the midst of a storm. You are my way maker in the midst of having no way. You are my heart fixer in the midst of a broken heart. You are my comfort in the midst of things uncomfortable. I love You Lord and I praise You.

I commit everything to You, show me any area of my life where I am not being obedient to Your will, You have my COMPLETE attention. I give You complete control with no fear. I want to be more and more like You daily. I worship You Lord. **(Isaiah 12:4-6)-" And in that day shall ye say, Praise the LORD, call upon his name, declare his doings among the people, make mention that his name is exalted. Sing unto the LORD; for he hath done excellent things: this is known in all the earth. Cry out and shout, thou inhabitant of Zion: for great is the Holy One of Israel in the midst of thee." (1Peter 1:3-9) "Blessed be the God and Father of our Lord Jesus Christ, which according to his abundant mercy hath begotten us again unto a lively hope by the resurrection of Jesus Christ from the dead, To an inheritance incorruptible, and undefiled, and that fadeth not away, reserved in heaven for you, Who are kept by the power of God through faith unto salvation ready to be revealed in the last time. Wherein ye greatly rejoice, though now for a season, if need be, ye are in**

heaviness through manifold temptations: That the trial of your faith, being much more precious than of gold that perisheth, though it be tried with fire, might be found unto praise and honour and glory at the appearing of Jesus Christ: Whom having not seen, ye love; in whom, though now ye see him not, yet believing, ye rejoice with joy unspeakable and full of glory: Receiving the end of your faith, even the salvation of your souls."

I pray: that we walk in our: NEW BIRTH, LIVING HOPE, INHERITANCE and FAITH, that we allow God to SHIELD us with His POWER, that we GREATLY REJOICE in the midst of our SUFFERING and TRIALS (that will only last a LITTLE while), that we continue to build our FAITH that has GREATER WORTH than GOLD, PROVE our FAITH to be more and more GENUINE daily, that the result might be PRAISE, GLORY and HONOR. FAITH comes by hearing.

I pray: that we walk by faith and not by sight, that we BELIEVE in the unSEEN, just as we BELIEVE and LOVE Jesus who we do not SEE, that one of our greatest desires is to be FILLED with more of Him so that we may be complete and overflowing with INEXPRESSIBLE and GLORIOUS JOY. To GOD be the GLORY!

Additional References: Isaiah 2:3, Ps.25:12

Reflections:

Our Dwelling Place

~~~

God is good and all the time He is good. I place my complete trust in Him and know that He is able to do all things. I praise Him and worship Him in spite of my circumstances. He is worthy of praise. Great is His faithfulness. **(Ps. 103:1-2, 5,8)** **"Bless the LORD, O my soul: and all that is within me, bless his holy name. Bless the LORD, O my soul, and forget not all his benefits: Who satisfieth thy mouth with good things; so that thy youth is renewed like the eagle's. The LORD is merciful and gracious, slow to anger, and plenteous in mercy."**

I pray: for the restoration of our souls, for God to give us a clean heart and a right spirit, for Him to do exceedingly, abundantly above all that we could ever imagine, that we would stand firm on His word and not allow ourselves to be tempted to faint in our wilderness, that we stand in the wilderness on His promises and when we can't stand we kneel worshiping Him for the promises to strengthen us to get back up again, that we dwell in the arms of our loving Father who has promised to **(Hebrews 13:5b)** **"for he hath said, I will never leave thee, nor forsake thee."** **(Ps. 90:1)** **"Lord, you have been our dwelling place throughout all generations."**

I pray that when we are weak that we would dwell in the arms of our loving Father who has told us that He will **(Exodus 15:13)** **"with his unfailing love lead you, and** with his strength he will guide you to his dwelling place." **(Ps. 91:1-2) "He that dwelleth in the secret place of the most High shall abide under the shadow of the Almighty. I will say of the LORD, He is my refuge and my fortress: my God; in him will I trust. "** I pray that when trouble has surrounded us and we can see nothing through the trouble, that we continue to listen, that we dwell in the arms of our Father who the word has said is our **(Ps. 32:7) "Thou art my hiding place; thou shalt preserve me from trouble; thou shalt compass me about with songs of deliverance."** So, now we ask: **(Ps. 15:1-5) "LORD, who shall abide in thy tabernacle? who shall dwell in thy holy hill? He that walketh uprightly, and worketh righteousness, and speaketh the truth in his heart. He that backbiteth not with his tongue, nor doeth evil to his neighbour, nor taketh up a reproach against his neighbour. In whose eyes a vile person is contemned; but he honoureth them that fear the LORD. He that sweareth to his own hurt, and changeth not. He that putteth not out his money to usury, nor taketh reward against the innocent. He that doeth these things shall never be moved."** To God be the Glory.

<u>**Additional References:**</u> 1Kings 8:30, 39, 2 Chronicles 6:2

<u>**Reflections:**</u>

Power of the Tongue

~

(Ps. 47:1) "O clap your hands, all ye people; shout unto God with the voice of triumph." (Ps. 48:1) "Great is the LORD, and greatly to be praised in the city of our God, in the mountain of his holiness." Therefore, since we are receiving a kingdom that cannot be shaken, let us be thankful, and so worship God acceptably with reverence and awe, for our (Hebrews 12:29) "God is a consuming fire."

I pray: that God will give us greater understanding of whom we are regardless of our circumstances right now. Nothing can stop God's plans for us, not even us, that we trust Him and speak into existence the promises of God. God has given us POWER in our tongue. (Mark 11:23) "For verily I say unto you, That whosoever shall say unto this mountain, Be thou removed, and be thou cast into the sea; and shall not doubt in his heart, but shall believe that those things which he saith shall come to pass; he shall have whatsoever he saith."

What are you believing for? Is it in line with God's will? As you wait for it are you following His directions on what your part is to get it? Are you walking in faith, believing that it is already done, trusting God to bring it into existence, keeping your mind stayed on Him and not how long you've waited? Are you speaking against it, OR are you speaking as if it's already yours. **(Ephesians 4:29) "Let no corrupt communication proceed out of your mouth, but that which is good to the use of edifying, that it may minister grace unto the hearers." (1John 5:14-15) "And this is the confidence that we have in him, that, if we ask any thing according to his will, he heareth us: And if we know that he hear us, whatsoever we ask, we know that we have the petitions that we desired of him." (John 14:13-14) "And whatsoever ye shall ask in my name, that will I do, that the Father may be glorified in the Son. If ye shall ask any thing in my name, I will do it."** Pray, ask in His name according to His will and listen to God as He responds to you, walk away in obedience to His reply, believing what you asked for will be given to you. **(2Timothy 1:7) "For God hath not given us the spirit of fear; but of power, and of love, and of a sound mind."**

I pray that we are all prepared to be worked on as God responds to our prayers. What we have asked for may require us to be prepared: to be humbled, to have Godly character built in us or to be shaped into the role we have asked for.

I pray for preparation of our soul, realization of our power and greater expectations of life that God has said He wants us to live life to the fullest having abundance. To God be the GLORY!

<u>**Additional References**</u>: 2Corinthians 10:5, Romans 8:37

<u>**Reflections:**</u>

Prayer

≈

Prepare your hearts for prayer, clear your minds for purity, and rest in this moment knowing that the next one will be a moment of expectancy for greatness to evolve.

God,

We come to You today with humble hearts, with spirits that want to be right in Your eyes. We know that having the joy of just being in Your presence is our strength. God, you woke us up this morning and got us out of bed, now what would You have us to do? Because if it were left up to us sometimes the circumstances of the world make it too hard to get out of bed, too hard to move past what we think and feel, too hard to press through the opinions of people.

God we recognize You as Lord over our lives, we know that You are not a man that You should lie. So, we remind You today of Your promises, we remind You of what You promised to be in our lives, our ever-present help, our dwelling place, our peace, our strength, our redeemer. Lord, we are open for you to do great work in us.

(Genesis 18:14) "IS THERE ANYTHING TOO DIFFI-CULT FOR GOD"

<u>ABSOLUTELY NOT!!!!</u>

To God be the Glory!

<u>Reflections:</u>

Let's go Deeper

∽

I will bless the Lord at all times and His praises shall continually be in my mouth. I magnify His name because He is so worthy, magnify Him with me, if it had not been for God on my side where would I be?

I thank Him for the anointing that He has placed on my life. I thank Him for the opportunity to pray with you. It is truly all about God. Thank you Lord. I thank God for choosing me, as His vessel and I know that behind every word is His voice that I listen and adhere to daily. God deserves the Glory, Honor and Praise. I am an obedient servant seeking to do His will. IT IS ALL ABOUT HIM! **(Ps. 31:14) "But I trusted in thee, O LORD: I said, Thou art my God."**

I pray that we seek God for a deeper relationship in Him. God's desire for all of us is that we become more and more dependent on Him. He wants to take us to places that we have never been. In order to get to those places we must go through the low valleys, treacherous mountains and narrow paths.

I pray that the Lord will keep us, strengthen us and give us direction. God's way is not easy but it is worth it. **(Hebrews 12:2-3) "Looking unto Jesus the author and finisher of our faith; who for the joy that was set before him endured the cross, despising the shame, and is set down at the right hand of the throne of God. For consider him that endured such contradiction of sinners against**

himself, lest ye be wearied and faint in your minds."
I pray that God will grow us up in Him. I pray: that we will not wander around in the wilderness, having to go through the same area over and over again because we refuse to see, can't see, or ignore what God is trying to teach us, that God will give us a teachable heart, an understanding mind, a keen/seeking eye, a listening ear and an unwavering faith. Walk with Him, walk to the deeper place that He has predestined you for. **(Hebrews 10:36) "For ye have need of patience, that, after ye have done the will of God, ye might receive the promise."**
I pray that we live what we believe, walk in wholeness ready to achieve and stay focused and open to receive. **(Philippians 3:13-14) "Brethren, I count not myself to have apprehended: but this one thing I do, forgetting those things which are behind, and reaching forth unto those things which are before, I press toward the mark for the prize of the high calling of God in Christ Jesus." (Ecclesiastes 3:1) "To everything there is a season, and a time to every purpose under the heaven."** To GOD be the GLORY!!!!!!!!

Additional References: Galatians 5:16, Ps27:14, Deuteronomy 1:6-7

Reflections:

Keep Walking

(Exodus 15:1-2)" Then sang Moses and the children of Israel this song unto the LORD, and spake, saying, I will sing unto the LORD, for he hath triumphed gloriously: the horse and his rider hath he thrown into the sea. The LORD is my strength and song, and he is become my salvation: he is my God, and I will prepare him an habitation; my father's God, and I will exalt him." (Exodus 15:11) "Who is like unto thee, O LORD, among the gods? who is like thee, glorious in holiness, fearful in praises, doing wonders?" (Hebrews 13:15-16) "By him therefore let us offer the sacrifice of praise to God continually, that is, the fruit of our lips giving thanks to his name. But to do good and to communicate forget not: for with such sacrifices God is well pleased." GLORY ALLELUIA! PRAISE HIM! It is Him who is worthy of all my praise. I rest in Him as I obediently seek to do His will that is above mine. God is Awesome and Worthy!!

I pray: that we have a complete understanding of the power of God in us, that we hook our tongue up with our faith and realize the unstoppable power of our God. He has created and made us for such a time as this and it is in this time I believe that God has our blessings right over our head ready to wash us in them. He's just waiting for us to walk by what we have heard from Him. As we walk we will come to the place He wants us to be and He will pour those blessings over us. BUT we MUST walk blindly and boldly. We are almost there. Keep walking through that wilderness and keep speaking as you walk. The Lord will give you one little blessing after the other to keep you encouraged on your way.

Keep walking. As you walk over those barriers that Satan has put in place for you ask God to continue to strengthen you, don't try to walk in your own strength because when you do you will fall, but get back up again, repent and ask God for His unfailing, unbreakable strength. You can do all things through Christ who strengthens you.

Keep walking even when the tears blur your vision. **(Ps.30:5) "Weeping may endure for a night, but Joy cometh in the morning."**

Keep walking even when fear begins to set in because it is so dark and you can't see any light in your path. **(2Chronicles 20:15) "Thus saith the LORD unto you, Be not afraid nor dismayed by reason of this great multitude; for the battle is not yours, but God's."**

Keep walking even when it feels like you have lost everything that you started out with, your friends, family, finances, and/or husband/boyfriend. **(Genesis 50:20) " You intended to harm me, but God intended it for good to accomplish what is now being done."** Keep walking even if every step you take it feels lonelier than the last one. **(Hebrews 13:5b) "for he hath said, I will never leave thee, nor forsake thee."**

Keep walking even when you feel overwhelmed with exhaustion worrying about how you are going to make it to the place that God has for you when you feel like you can't walk another step. **(1Peter 5:7) "Casting all your care upon him; for he careth for you."**

Keep walking even when you have no joy and ask God to give you joy and stay focused on where you are going, what you heard, what He has promised you. We can walk in joy even when we can't see. We can hear, we can believe and walk in who we are even before we can see it, even before in the fleshly eyes we get there. Walk in the joy of the Lord. Walk in the joy of where you are, verses where you were. Walk in the joy of who you are and who you used to be. **(Ps. 37:4) "Delight thyself also in the LORD; and he shall give thee the desires of thine heart."** KEEP WALKING! PUSH YOURSELF! KEEP WALKING! Whether you turn to the right or to the left, your ears will hear a voice behind you saying, **(Isaiah 30:21) "And thine ears shall hear a word behind thee, saying, This is the way, walk ye in it, when ye turn to the right hand, and when ye turn to the left."** (Romans 12:12) "Rejoicing in hope; patient in tribulation; continuing instant in prayer"** Claim it VICTORY is YOURS! To God be the GLORY!!!!!!

Additional References: Colossians 2:10, 2Corinthians 5:17,Habakkuk 3:19

Reflections:

Go to the Word

How ow sweet it is to be wrapped in the arms of the one who promises to **(Hebrews 13:5b) "for he hath said, I will never leave thee, nor forsake thee."** I love Him because He first loved me. He loved me in spite of myself what an awesome wonder He is. My God, my Father, He is all that I need and everything that I want. He is a way maker when things look impossible. He shows me how possible things actually are. I thank Him because if it had not been for Him I would have lost my mind in the hands of the things and people of this world.

God has brought me through things that should have killed me but His plans for me are so much greater and I need Him. I need Him to breathe life into me. I need Him to be the first person that speaks to me in the morning. Every morning my spirit wakes up, singing a song, in my mind to Him of my love, gratefulness, joy and appreciation. He is the center and focal point of my life, the lover of my soul, the Father who has freed me and made me whole. I worship Him in spite of what things look like in the world, in spite of what people say and in spite of my circumstances. He is truly worthy. I love Him forever and ever. **(Ps. 64: 10) "The righteous shall be glad in the LORD, and shall trust in him; and all the upright in heart shall glory."**

God's word has given us every answer that we need. It has provided us every direction that we should take, in every

231

circumstance that life brings before us. When we are lonely we should go to the word. **(Isaiah 41:9-10) "Thou whom I have taken from the ends of the earth, and called thee from the chief men thereof, and said unto thee, Thou art my servant; I have chosen thee, and not cast thee away. Fear thou not; for I am with thee: be not dismayed; for I am thy God: I will strengthen thee; yea, I will help thee."** When no one and nothing can help us out of a troubled situation, we should go to the word **(Isaiah 43:2) "When thou passest through the waters, I will be with thee; and through the rivers, they shall not overflow thee: when thou walkest through the fire, thou shalt not be burned; neither shall the flame kindle upon thee."** When we are plagued with a guilty conscience, we should go to the word. **(Hebrews 10:22) "Let us draw near with a true heart in full assurance of faith, having our hearts sprinkled from an evil conscience, and our bodies washed with pure water"** When we are being attacked, we should go to the word **(2Timothy 4:18) "And the Lord shall deliver me from every evil work, and will preserve me unto his heavenly kingdom: to whom be glory for ever and ever. Amen."** To God be the Glory!

<u>**Reflections:**</u>

It's in the Word

God is an awesome God and He is worthy to be praised. The God who is the center of my life, the hope in my heart, the joy in my smile, the peace in my presence, and the comfort in my circumstances, the lover of my soul responsible for making me whole, He is my slow drag partner, the one who has His arms wrapped around me in the midst of my loneliness. I can feel His presence, loving me and showing me that I am special. He is mighty, He is wonderful, He is my all and all and all!

I praise Him because when I think about the ways in which He has changed my thinking and how He has changed my heart, it gives me a wealth of confidence. **(Ps.107:1) "O Give thanks unto the Lord, for he is good: for his mercy endureth for ever."**

I pray that we allow God to change our thinking. If our thoughts are filled with doubt then we should go to the word and change those thoughts, speak to ourselves, tell our soul about what God has put in the word just for us right in that very doubting moment. **(Ps. 20:7-8) "Some trust in chariots, and some in horses: but we will remember the name of the LORD our God. They are brought down and fallen: but we are risen, and stand upright."**

When things look impossible, remind yourself of the word **(Ps. 31:14-15a) "But I trusted in thee, O LORD: I said, Thou art my God. My times are in your hands."**

When your mind is filled with fear remind yourself of the word. **(Ps. 56:3-4) "When I am afraid, I will trust thee. In God I will praise his word, in God I have put my trust; I will not fear what flesh can do unto me." (Philippians 4:7) "And the peace of God, which passeth all understanding, shall keep your hearts and minds through Christ Jesus." (Isaiah 51:12-13,16) "I, even I, am he that comforteth you: who art thou, that thou shouldest be afraid of a man that shall die, and of the son of man which shall be made as grass; And forgettest the LORD thy maker, that hath stretched forth the heavens, and laid the foundations of the earth; and hast feared continually every day because of the fury of the oppressor, as if he were ready to destroy? and where is the fury of the oppressor? And I have put my words in thy mouth, and I have covered thee in the shadow of mine hand, that I may plant the heavens, and lay the foundations of the earth, and say unto Zion, Thou art my people."**

When your mind is filled with sorrow and you are feeling weak, remind yourself of the word. **(Isaiah 51:9-11) "Awake, awake, put on strength, O arm of the LORD; awake, as in the ancient days, in the generations of old. Art thou not it that hath cut Rahab, and wounded the dragon? Art thou not it which hath dried the sea, the waters of the great deep; that hath made the depths of the sea a way for the ransomed to pass over? Therefore the redeemed of the LORD shall return, and come with singing unto Zion; and everlasting joy shall be upon their head: they shall obtain gladness and joy; and sorrow and mourning shall flee away. "**

Whatever we need is in His word, whatever we want is in His word, what ever we are going through, someone in the word has went through, and it is up to us to use those people as examples of how to go through or how not to go through. Teach us, testify **Naomi**, (the book of Ruth) whose husband

and sons died and she felt like she was left alone, but she was left with a daughter-in-law (Ruth) who she couldn't appreciate until they went through some stuff together. Teach us, testify **Ruth**, who lost her husband but saw God, a God she was not familiar with, in the eyes of her mother- in-law before the tragedies of death plagued them both. She was determined to stay close to her mother-in-law to see Him again. Teach us, testify **Rahab**, who lived as a prostitute but who still knew how to make right choices. Teach us, testify **Paul**, who killed Christians and then one day God showed up in His life and from that moment on he was never the same. As he sat in prison he wrote a large portion of the New Testament.

Teach us, testify **David**, who was a liar, murderer, and adulterer but God said was " a man after His own Heart" (see Psalms where most of David's heart was written into words). It's in the word and the people who went through some of the same things that we go through wrote it. God has given us the word to survive through life because we are not the first to have troubles and we won't be the last. So, as they went through for us we must go through for others, that our testimony will free others from thinking they are all alone. We are never alone, we might think we are alone, but we are never alone. To GOD BE THE GLORY!

Additional References: The book of Ruth, Acts, Galatians, Ephesians 1&2 Corinthians

Reflections:

Gifts of Life

~~~

*L*ife is a gift. Life is beautiful. God breathes life into us. He breathes life into us daily. His breath ignites and develops gifts that only we can deliver, master and call our own. Each and every one of us who call ourselves His children, who call Him our Savior, are filled with gifts.

In order to allow God to develop these gifts we must pray daily. Pray that God would breathe life into us, and life more abundantly into us, that we would inhale the grace of God and exhale the troubles of life that sometimes take our breath away.

God says cast your cares on Him. As you do breathe in, take the breath that He freely gives. As you breathe in allow Him to fill you up with the breath that will develop your gifts that will allow you to walk the walk of life with out giving up.

To walk and not faint, to run and not get weary, to finish the race of life without getting tired, without losing your strength because the joy of the Lord is your strength.

As He breathes into you and develops your gifts, He strengthens you to deliver those gifts to people all around you with little effort. He strengthens you to master those gifts as you learn that without His breath you can do nothing.

So you become a master at the gifts that He has given you and that you've allowed Him to master through you. He strengthens you to accept and call your gift " Your Gift" while giving Him the Glory for it, knowing that without Him you are nothing.

Life's purpose is to know your purpose, that you might accept, respect and identify the gifts that God has given you. The gifts He has made you to be for another one of His children.

In every season of our life we are something for someone. Rather it's warmth in the cold of the winter or shade in the heat of the summer, or a beautiful leaf to drop into there fall or a blossoming flower to bloom in the spring.

In every season of life, everyone needs a gift from God. Daily we breathe in God's gift of breath, so daily we should allow our life to be someone's gift. To God be the GLORY!

Thank You for Reading

_This is the day that the Lord has made I choose to rejoice and be glad. Oh Magnify the Lord with me because He is worthy to be praised. Taste and see that the Lord is good and He works all things together for our good. I will bless the Lord at all times and His praises shall continually be in my mouth. I'm thankful that I have found a place in Him, a place to glorify, magnify and edify my soul. My soul says yes to all of His requests.

I'm thankful that I serve a GOD bigger than my finances, bigger than my circumstances, bigger than my trials, bigger than my tribulations. He is worthy to be praised. I want more, more and more of Him. I need so much more. I need Him to fill my cup that has been so empty for so long. I want it to overflow with His love. I have grabbed a hold of this love and allowed it to absorb into every area of my life. I am a sponge soaking up more and more of Him daily. I am a blooming flower becoming more and more beautiful on the inside flowing over to the outside. It is all about Him. He shines His light upon me. It is that light shining so bright that if you don't know Him you are unable to bear the glare and not have a desire to know Him. If you know Him you recognize the shine. God is an awesome God.

I thank Him for every single person whose eyes read these prayers. I thank Him that He has anointed me to speak the truth of His words with boldness, clarity, knowledge and experience. God is a good God. He has created us to be no respecter of persons, to see people and look for Him in them. He has given me the gift to meet people where they are and help to get them where He wants them to be. I thank Him that He has deemed me worthy. I thank Him for His favor and I thank Him that He has given you to me for such a time as this. It is time to listen and respond in action to the word that we have heard from God. It is time to grow up, stand up and reach up. God is available any time, anywhere and anyhow. He doesn't care how we come, He just wants us to come. **(2Corinthians 12:7-10) " And lest I should be exalted above measure through the abundance of the revelations, there was given to me a thorn in the flesh, the messenger of Satan to buffet me, lest I should be exalted above measure. For this thing I besought the Lord thrice, that it might depart from me. And he said unto me, My grace is sufficient for thee: for my strength is made perfect in weakness. Most gladly therefore will I rather glory in my infirmities, that the power of Christ may rest upon me. Therefore I take pleasure in infirmities, in reproaches, in necessities, in persecutions, in distresses for Christ's sake: for when I am weak, then am I strong."** I thank God for Jesus and I thank Him for all of you.

Lets Seal This With a Prayer

Pray with me:

 *L*ord, we thank You for Your unfailing love. We thank You for every word that has come out of this book that has met us right where we are to help us get to where we are going. We thank You that in spite of ourselves You love us, there is no one greater than You and as shared in these words there is no one more responsible for these words and the fact that we are reading them then YOU, LORD.

Lord thank You, thank You that even when we have not been obedient to You, You still allowed us to dwell in the sanctuary of Your arms. We thank You that You are merciful and we ask You to make us stronger in You so that we may be more and more like You daily, that we may do all that You ask us to do in spite of our circumstances and that we will be more and more obedient to do Your will. In the mighty name of Jesus we pray this prayer and ask You to prepare our hearts. God we know that You know our hearts.

I pray that we know Your hearts just as well as You know ours. God we know that You do not give us assignments to make our lives comfortable. You give us assignments for the building of the Kingdom. So we step out today of our comfort zone to do Your will and watch the rewards of You, OUR proud FATHER.

We love You Lord!

Printed in the United States
50517LVS00001B/106-336

9 781597 818186